Suffolk Walks with Children

Cyril Francis

Published by Sigma Leisure – an imprint of
Sigma Press, 1 South Oak Lane, Wilmslow, Cheshire SK9 6AR, England.

British Library Cataloguing in Publication Data
A CIP record for this book is available from the British Library.

ISBN: 1-85058-771-X

Cover photographs: clockwise, from bottom left – Ramsholt church; Thorpeness Mill; Lavenham *(Ikon imaging)*; Orwell Country Park *(Cyril Francis)*

Photographs: Cyril Francis

Maps: Jeremy Semmens

Typesetting and Design by: Sigma Press, Wilmslow, Cheshire.

Printed by: MFP Design & Print

Disclaimer: the information in this book is given in good faith and is believed to be correct at the time of publication. No responsibility is accepted by either the author or publisher for errors or omissions, or for any loss or injury howsoever caused. Only you can judge your own fitness, competence and experience.

For Callum & Caitlin

Foreword

Just as I was preparing this book, practically the whole country was in the grip of a foot and mouth epidemic. In Suffolk, a few paths remained open but the majority were closed. Trying to plan a circular walk was nigh impossible. When the restrictions were finally lifted, I began to research the book in earnest. As each walk progressed I found the task of looking for items to be included on the checklist and searching for clues on which to base the questions, very rewarding. During the process, I made one or two discoveries of my own of objects which I never knew existed beforehand. I have tried to include something for all age groups. I hope that the answers won't prove too difficult or for that matter, too easy. Do I already hear groans or sighs of satisfaction (arguments too, probably) as each final score is added up?

Looking back, I see that I've included lots of water in one form or other on the walks, purely unintentionally at the outset. Arguably, walking along a cliff-top path overlooking the North Sea provides a refreshing change from some boring field-edge paths. As does a view from the riverbank of sailing yachts and dinghies; following a stretch of the River Stour as it meanders through lush meadowland or simply paddling in a shallow roadside ford – all are featured in the book. Elsewhere there is the opportunity to walk along one of Britain's oldest roads – the Icknield Way. Using a combination of paths and dismantled railway lines you can explore Medieval towns such as Lavenham, Clare and Hadleigh, made prosperous at one time by the wool and cloth industries. A short detour from the route enables you to visit Sudbury with its Gainsborough connections or historic Woodbridge.

All the routes follow public rights of way and most are well waymarked. I have quoted the use of OS Explorer maps but Landranger and Pathfinder will do as well. Anyone wanting public transport should telephone 0870 608 2 608 for further details.

Finally a word for the children: please let the adults join in the fun and you won't cheat, will you? Happy walking!

Cyril Francis

Contents

Quick Reference

Plan your day at a glance with this chart and the location map which follows, to check which routes have the features or facilities you require. For more information, see the individual route.

Notes and Key

Bus: routes that start within a short distance of a bus stop

Café: café or tea room along the route or very close to it

Pub: pub along the route where families are welcome

Wet Weather: routes with hard surface all the way round, suitable for all weather conditions

Flat: route is more or less flat, little climbing required

Historical: places or features of historical interest along the route

Pushchairs: walks with at least part of the route suitable for pushchairs

Features: places of specific interest to families along the route

	Bus	Café	Pub	Flat	Historical	Pushchairs	Features
1. Barham & Baylham	✓		✓			✓	Picnic site, fishing lakes and scenic views
2. Beyton	✓		✓	✓		✓	Village green and arable fields
3. Clare	✓	✓	✓		✓	✓	Country Park, castle ruins and former railway station
4. East Bergholt	✓	✓	✓		✓	✓	Fine views, river stretch and water meadows
5. Eye	✓	✓	✓	✓	✓	✓	Castle ruins, church, guildhall and countryside
6. Felixstowe - Landguard Point	✓	✓	✓		✓	✓	Embankments, beach, sea, old fort and port viewing area
7. Gazeley, Dalham & Moulton			✓		✓		Woodland, an old malt kiln and a packhorse bridge
8. Hadleigh	✓	✓	✓	✓	✓	✓	Former rail track, arable fields and historic town
9. Harleston, Shelland & Onehouse	✓						Picnic site, woodland and unusual church
10. Hoxne	✓		✓		✓	✓	Large village. Legend of St Edmund
11. Lavenham	✓	✓	✓	✓	✓	✓	Magnificent church, timber-framed houses and former railway line
12. Needham Market	✓	✓	✓	✓		✓	Large lake and river path
13. Orwell Country Park						✓	Picnic site, woodland and Orwell Bridge
14. Pin Mill			✓	✓			Stretch of river, woods and excellent views
15. Polstead			✓		✓		Village famous for Red Barn murder. Undulating paths
16. Sizewell		✓	✓			✓	Beach, cliffs. Thorpeness village
17. Southwold	✓	✓	✓	✓	✓	✓	Harbour, marshes, new pier, beach and lighthouse
18. Sudbury	✓			✓	✓	✓	Valley walk and water meadows. Picnic site
19. Witnesham	✓		✓				Arable farmland. Good views
20. Woodbridge	✓	✓	✓		✓	✓	Riverside walk and woodland

Location Map

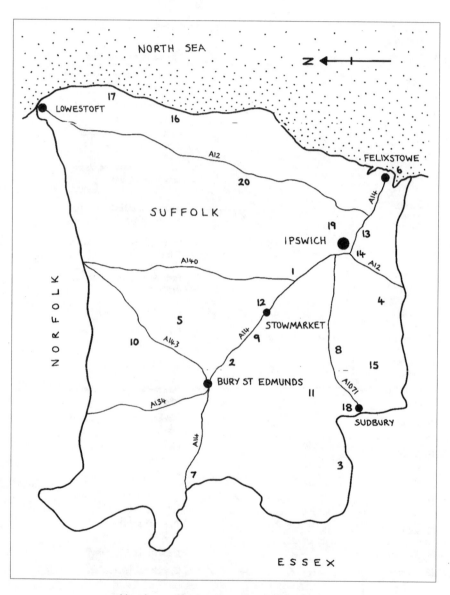

Numbers refer to approximate locations;
see previous page for features and facilities

Welcome to Suffolk

Although this book has children very much in mind, it is written for families and anyone who is young at heart. The twenty circular walks might be described as a series of treasure hunts on foot. Each walk has a list of questions to be answered, with points awarded for each correct answer. Historic churches, old buildings, an inland lighthouse, a centuries-old packhorse bridge and a modem equivalent, a tide mill and some castle ruins, are just some of the many subjects which feature in the search for clues. On the routes, you might be walking along a former railway line, on a coastal path, beside a slow moving river, or in the footsteps of famous painters such as Constable and Gainsborough.

Walks are of varying distances and mostly start from country parks or official picnic sites, some of which contain toilet facilities. Details of where you may obtain light refreshments are also included, which hopefully will add to your enjoyment.

Each walk may be a considered a challenge, but one not to be taken too seriously. Children should try to answer each question and keep their eyes open for clues. A day spent in the Suffolk countryside should be one of recreation and enjoyment; rewarded in the knowledge that you have discovered some interesting facets about this delightful county.

Introductory Notes

This is a very unusual book, intended to be read by both parents and children. The following conventions have been used to make the book as useful as possible to both categories.

⇨ Directions are clearly displayed in this style of text, so that they can be seen at a glance.

☺ Information for the children is set in a contrasting typestyle. This can be read aloud, or children can read it for themselves.

Q1. Questions are in this typestyle (answers are at the back of the book).

There are points for each correct answer. You don't have to score points, but many children (and grown-ups!) enjoy the extra challenge. Make a note of the scores along the walk.

Checklists appear at the start of each walk, for children to tick off things as they see them. If you do not want to write in the book, copy the checklist onto a piece of paper and give one to each child, so they can compete to see who spots the most.

The total score is the total of the points awarded to questions and for things spotted in the checklist. At the end of the walk there are some comments on the likely scores – but don't take them too seriously!

Public Transport and Tourist Information Centres

There are about 40 different bus companies operating around Suffolk so the most appropriate contact for general bus information is the **National Travel Line**, telephone 0870 608 2 608 and for **Rail Enquiries** telephone 08457 48 49 50. However, for more specific regional information the **Tourist Information Centres** can be contacted in the following areas:

Aldeburgh	01728 453637	
Beccles	01502 713196	
Brandon	01842 814955	
Bury St Edmunds	01284 764667	
Felixstowe	01394 276770	
Ipswich	01473 258070	
Lavenham	01787 248207	*(Apr – Oct only)*
Lowestoft	01502 533600	
Newmarket	01638 667200	
Southwold	01502 724729	
Stowmarket	01449 676800	
Sudbury	01787 881320	
Woodbridge	01394 382240	

Note: an excellent leaflet, "A Day Out in Suffolk", can be obtained from Tourist Information Centres. This gives brief details of just about every attraction in the county, together with opening times and admission charges. Information is also available on the Suffolk County Council web site: www.suffolkcc.gov.uk/tourism

Walk 1. Barham & Baylham

Barham picnic site with its central position along the Gipping Valley, is an ideal spot to start this walk. The site has picnic tables, a children's play area and toilet facilities. A small exhibition room explains the industrial history of the valley and the present aim of promoting recreation and conservation. The area is rich in mineral deposits. Sand and gravel have been extracted for supply to the building industry. Pits, which are now dug out, have been stocked with fish. As a result, Barham Pits is a popular attraction for anglers. Later, the walk takes you to the villages of Great Blakenham and Baylham. The latter's position on a high ridge overlooking the valley gives extended views across the local countryside.

Some pretty, thatched cottages with stone walls stand either side of the road before you descend the fruity sounding, Plum Pudding Hill. Baylham Mill is an 18th-century building, which was one of a number of mills that once worked alongside the River Gipping. The ancient Roman site of Combretovium – a fort and small town – is now home to a rare-breeds farm. At Baylham House (just off the route) you will find breeding groups of cattle, sheep, pigs, goats and poultry. A delightful riverside walk takes you back to your starting point.

Starting Point: Barham picnic site is just off the old Ipswich – Norwich Road. Turn up Pest House Lane and follow the road round. Grid Reference: TM126 512.

Parking: Car park at Barham picnic site.

Distance: 5 miles.

Map: OS Explorer No 211 Bury St Edmunds and Stowmarket.

Terrain: Easy paths, mostly on the level but with one or two up and downhill sections.

Pushchairs: Suitable mainly for picnic site area and river path.

Public Toilets: Available at picnic site.

Refreshments: Tables available at site for a picnic. The Chequers pub in Great Blakenham does children's meals and has a small play area.

Checklist: score 2 points for each

1. A wooden fence
2. A rabbit
3. A fishing rod – there should be plenty of these if there is a fishing match
4. A telephone box
5. A magpie
6. Some rusting farm machinery
7. A line of electricity pylons
8. A post-box
9. A village hall
10. Some water lilies
11. A kestrel
12. A wooden seat

Total Score: _____

The Walk

⇨   Leave the car park, turn left past the toilet block and continue on a tarmac path to a children's play area.

☺   Why not spend some time when you return on the swings and climbing frame?

⇨   Go through a gate, up and down some steps over an embankment and turn left. Carry on beside a wooden fence to reach a flooded gravel pit. Bear right and proceed along a path with some pits on the left to reach a large board signed Barham B Pit.

Q1 Study the board and decide what the letters GAPS stand for.

Score 2 points.

☺   Some days there are several fishermen on the banks trying patiently to hook a fish. You may get a close-up view of a fish being caught or one being landed with a net.

⇨   Turn left here, passing more water-filled pits on the left until you face a large shed a short distance away in front. Turn right here to pass under

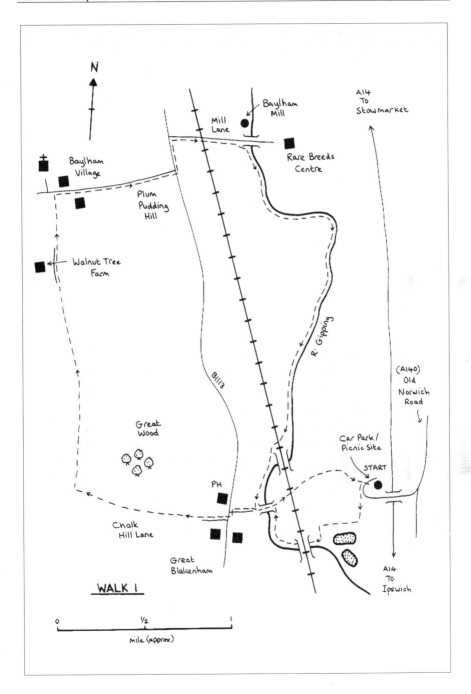

N

Baylham Mill

Mill Lane

A14 To Stowmarket

Rare Breeds Centre

Baylham Village

Plum Pudding Hill

Walnut Tree Farm

R. Gipping

(A140) Old Norwich Road

B1113

Car Park / Picnic Site

START

Great Wood

PH

Chalk Hill Lane

Great Blakenham

A14 To Ipswich

WALK 1

0   ½   1

mile (approx)

a railway bridge and emerge beside the River Gipping. Follow the river on the left and go over two stiles. Turn left and cross a brick bridge to join the surfaced Mill Lane. Follow the lane and soon bear right to reach the B1113 just ahead. Now look to your right.

Q2 What is the name of the public house?

Score 2 points.

⇨ Cross straight over the road with care and walk up Chalk Hill Lane. The area beneath the soil is covered in chalk, much of which was used at one time in the local manufacture of cement. Away to the left are large "dug-out" pits. Hence the appropriately named Chalk Hill Lane.

☺ As you approach a residential caravan site going off to the right, look for a sign just before the entrance.

Q3 What is the speed limit here?

Score 3 points.

⇨ The surfaced lane shortly turns into an unmade gravel track. Continue along the track and soon turn right onto a broad field track with a hedge on the left and an arable field on the right. Keep forward on the rising track to reach a small copse. Go through the copse and veer left to join a cross-field path and aim for a hedgerow at the field boundary.

⇨ If you cannot find this path, carry on down an adjacent broad track to finally reach a surfaced lane. Otherwise, when you reach the hedge go through a gate and head across some pasture. Go through another gate and turn left when you reach a lane. Immediately opposite Walnut Tree Farm turn sharp right and go down an earth track which in places provides a lovely tunnel effect. Turn right when you reach Baylham Village and start walking down the road. Go past the village hall and after about 150 metres look to your left for a sign on a farm building.

Q4 What colour and what type of corn is included in the name of this farm?

Score 2 points for each answer.

⇨ Carry on down Plum Pudding Hill to reach the junction with the B1113 again. Turn left here and after about 50 metres turn right into Mill Lane.

☺ After going over a railway crossing look for a road sign on the left.

**Q5 Which type of vehicle is not allowed beyond this point?
Score 2 points.**

▷ With the disused Baylham Mill on the left, turn right over a stile to join the Gipping Valley Foot Path. (If you wish to make a short detour and visit the Rare Breeds Farm, the entrance to Baylham House is just across the bridge in front of you.)

Baylham Mill

☺ You can see some of the animals from a vantage-point on the river path.

▷ Follow the riverside path for another mile or so, ignoring all paths going left. When you finally reach some rear gardens of houses and the path peters out, ignore a public footpath going right. Carry on for a few more metres, turn sharp right, go through an alleyway and turn left at the top. Turn left again and keep forward over a brick bridge, ignoring a path beside the river walked earlier.

▷ Veer left on a path which runs between pasture land on either side. Go over a stile and head towards the railway line in front. Cross the line with care by a stile either side, swing left and then right onto a sandy path. Continue to the end of the track, bear right and the picnic site is in front of you facing left.

―――――――――――――――

Now add up your score.

More than 28   Very impressive!

20 – 28   Keen eyes!

Less than 20   Not quite so good today!

Walk 2. Beyton

Beyton has some good paths, which take you around this small village and beyond. High hedgerows remain intact and a woodside stretch provides a pleasant interlude. A lovely triangular shaped green overlooks the village centre. Here a gaggle of geese wander – or should I say waddle – at will, leaving their feathers (and droppings) all over the place. How and when the geese initially arrived is something of a mystery, each generation succeeding the other perhaps. They appear to be visitor friendly and not averse to accepting the odd piece of bread. Their presence has been immortalised on the village sign. Passing the green on one side is the former main road to Bury St Edmunds.

Since the village was effectively bypassed by the building of the now A14, the traffic flow has lessened, making it more attractive to walkers and residents alike. While some other villages in Suffolk have lost their only remaining pub, Beyton has somehow managed to hold onto two, The White Horse and The Bear, positioned at either end of the green. All Saints church is unusual in that it has an oval shaped flint tower, probably Norman, which was buttressed in later years. Apparently, this type of tower is one of only two to be found in the county. Elsewhere in the village, references to Quaker Lane and Quaker Farm may suggest that the Society of Friends once had a presence here.

Starting Point: Beyton is just off the A14, 5 miles SE of Bury St Edmunds.

Parking: Beside the road in the SW corner of the green near the White Horse pub. Grid Reference: 935 634

Distance: 3 miles.

Map: OS Explorer No 211 Bury St Edmunds and Stowmarket.

Terrain: Easy walking on good paths, which may well become muddy during wet weather.

Pushchairs: Suitable only around the village green area.

Public Toilets: None.

Refreshments: The White Horse public house does home cooked food and has a garden with an amusement area for children. The Bear public house has a small garden and also welcomes children.

Checklist: score 2 points for each

1. A post box

2. A bus shelter

3. Some goose feathers

4. Iron railings near a stream

5. No's 1 & 2 Bramble Cottages

6. A holly hedge

7. A conifer hedge

8. A stagnant pond

9. A distant church tower – look left across some fields

10. Stinging nettles – loads of them!

11. Some steps on a telegraph pole

12. A butterfly

Total Score _____

The White Horse, Beyton

The Walk

⇨ Facing the White Horse public house turn left and with Beyton Green on the left, continue walking along the road until you reach the village sign.

Q1 How many geese are included on the sign?

Score 2 points.

☺ Have you come across the geese waddling around yet?

⇨ With the Bear Inn on the left, take the road signposted to Drinkstone. After about 500 metres turn right by a footpath sign and follow a field-edge path, which after 20 metres goes to the left of a hedge. Almost at the far end of the field bear right and go between a woven fence and a hedge to emerge into All Saints churchyard.

☺ Look for a lovely wooden bench positioned by the side of the church wall.

Q2 Which notable date has been crafted into the back of the bench?

Score 2 points.

⇨ Come out of the churchyard, cross straight over Church Road and continue along a narrow path starting beyond some concrete in front of you. Keep forward until you reach Quaker Lane and go straight over.

Q3 What is the name of the farm on the left-hand side?

Score 2 points.

⇨ Continue down a driveway, go through a metal gate and bear slightly right. The path runs beside an uncultivated field on the left to reach a hedge and then heads towards Chevin's Wood in front.

☺ A lovely paddock for horses has been created here. Look around the paddock and count the number of horses you can see.

⇨ When you reach the wood turn left, proceed along a grassy path and shortly enter another field. Where the wood finishes, swing right and continue beside the wood to the field boundary. Turn right here with a hedge

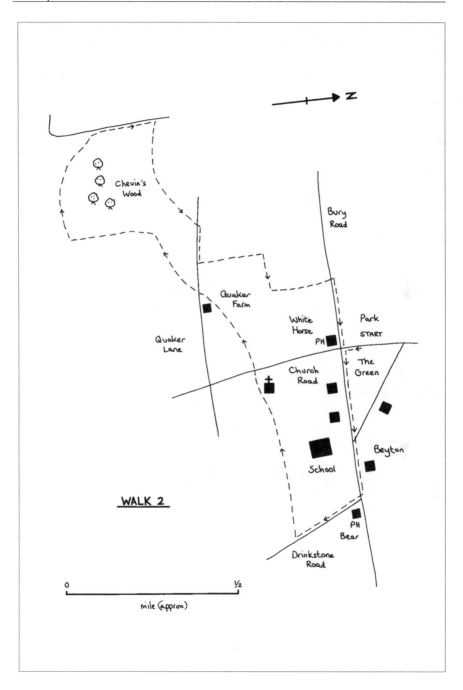

on the left and soon pass a lone oak tree on the right. Carry on heading towards a house in front and turn right when you reach a minor road.

⇨ After about 500 metres turn right onto a waymarked path with a hedge on the right. After about 150 metres veer left and take a cross-field path which goes to the corner of Chevin's Wood. (If this path is not evident, continue round the perimeter of the field.) Turn left when you reach the wood and continue on a field-edge path to reach Quaker Lane again.

⇨ Turn right here and carry on along the road. Just before you reach the first house, turn left down a grassy path with hedgerows either side. After about 30 metres look left and find a plaque attached to a tree trunk.

Q4 What is the name of the pond mentioned on the plaque?

Score 2 points.

⇨ Continue ahead on a field-edge path with a hedge on the right to eventually meet the old Bury Road. Go down some steps cut into the bank and cross a bridge over a stream. Turn right and follow the road back to your start point.

Q5 Think back – how many stiles did you cross? A "tricky" question this one!

Score 2 points.

Now add up your score.

28 – 34	You make it look easy!
20 – 27	A good effort!
Under 20	Sharpen your pencil a bit more!

Walk 3. Clare

Where is the only place in England where a railway station was built inside a castle? Answer: the small market town of Clare and in particular Clare Castle Country Park, from where this walk starts. The Norman castle was built towards the end of the 11th century. It's doubtful whether the castle saw a shot (sic) fired in anger. When it was no longer needed to guard the town, the castle fell into ruins. Following the Great Eastern Railway Company's decision to build a railway along the Stour Valley, permission was sought to run the line through the castle grounds. Buildings and platforms were later added and Clare Station was officially opened in 1865. Nowadays, the original goods shed has been converted into a visitor centre, which contains information on the park, castle and railway.

The park has plenty of space in which to move around, play games or take a picnic. You can take a spiral walk around the castle mound for a view of the town. Information boards posted at various intervals provide details of plants, birds and animals likely to be found within the park. After leaving the park, the compact walk skirts the town and you are seldom far from the centre. The lofty tower of the Gothic wool church of St Peter and St Paul acts as a local landmark, which is useful for the return journey. Standing at the corner of the churchyard (not on route) is Clare Ancient House. Its elaborate pargeting – high-relief plastic decoration – bears the date 1473 and makes the House one of the most celebrated examples of this form of folk decoration in the country.

Starting Point: Clare is on the A1092 between the A604 and the A134, 8 miles from Sudbury and 8 miles from Haverhill.

Parking: Clare Castle Country Park is just off the town centre and is open throughout the year.

Distance: 4 miles.

Map: OS Explorer No 210 Newmarket and Haverhill.

Terrain: Good paths and tracks with some uphill and downhill walking.

Pushchairs: Suitable only in and around the park.

Public Toilets: Some in the Country Park.

Refreshments: There is a fish and chip shop in the High Street. The Seafarer Pub in Nethergate Street has a garden and welcomes children.

Checklist: score 2 points for each

1. A dragonfly
2. A lifebelt
3. A swan
4. A river bridge
5. Townsend House
6. Some sheds on an allotment
7. A glider in the sky
8. Stour Valley path sign
9. A communications mast
10. A pigeon
11. Clare Priory sign
12. A rook

Total Score _____

The Walk

☺ Before the walk, take a look into the restored goods van and find the answer to the first question.

Q1 In which year did the railway close?

Score 2 points.

⇨ Leave the car park and take a surfaced path, which leads, down to the bank of the New Cut (River Stour). The path runs through some trees and close to the water. Shortly a large pond will appear on the left.

☺ Just before you cross a tarmac path, look to the right.

Q2 What artefact of the former railway still exists?

Score 2 points.

⇨ Continue ahead and then bear right onto a narrow surfaced path, which turns left in front of a house to emerge onto Cavendish Road. Turn right here, go over a bridge and cross the road. Turn left into Harp Lane, which runs alongside a playing field. Continue straight ahead to meet Eastfields Farm.

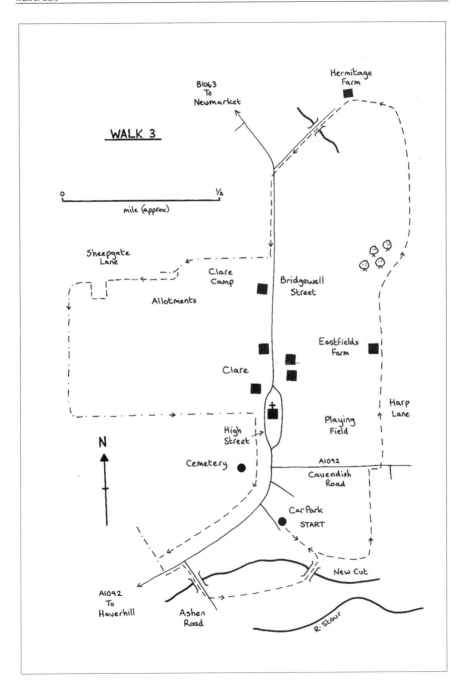

WALK 3

B1063
To
Newmarket

Hermitage
Farm

0   ½
mile (approx)

Sheepgate
Lane

Clare
Camp

Allotments

Bridgewell
Street

Eastfields
Farm

Clare

Harp
Lane

High
Street

N

Cemetery

Playing
Field

A1092
Cavendish
Road

Car Park

START

New Cut

A1092
To
Haverhill

Ashen
Road

R. Stour

☺ Take a close look at the farm building.

Q3 What farm animal is placed on top of the weather vane?

Score 2 points.

⇨ Keep the farm building on the left and just past a bungalow and poultry shed the path narrows to enter a belt of trees. After about 300 metres the path leads into a field. Turn left here and follow the field-edge with a hedge on the left to the field boundary.

☺ This field is mostly full of corn. Can you tell whether the crop is wheat, barley or perhaps sugar beet? There may be nothing growing at all, possibly left under what is termed set-aside land.

⇨ Turn left through a gap in the hedge and make for nearby Heritage Farm buildings. Fork left in front of a large barn to join a concrete road. Keep forward, pass over a stream and join an estate road with the B1063 road in front of you.

☺ Just before turning left onto the B1063, have a good look at a yellow and green marker badge, indicating the route of the Clare to Bury St Edmunds walk.

Q4 What emblem does the badge contain?

Score 2 points.

⇨ Walk along Bridgewell Street for about 200 metres and cross the road when you come level with a black timber shed. Continue straight up a rising track – a little bit of extra puff and bending of the back are needed here.

☺ This is an historical area known as Clare Camp; possibly the site of an Iron Age fort which may have been used by the Romans.

⇨ Ignore all paths going left. Just after the track bears right, pass left through a hedge gap into some garden allotments in front.

☺ Can you identify anything used by allotment holders to deter birds from picking seeds, pieces of plastic or foil attached to a length of string perhaps.

⇨ Bear right and continue on a path that now runs parallel with the track you have just left. Continue ahead and go left and right past a fenced compound. Keep on the field-edged path and eventually enter another field. Turn left onto a track with a hedge on the left and, when you reach a track junction, turn left and head back towards Clare, making for the church tower in the distance. At the bottom of the field, bear right and shortly arrive at the cemetery.

Clare church

☺ You are now at the dead centre of Clare – sorry, just a joke!

⇨ Pass the graveyard on the right, go over a stretch of grass and gravel and pass through a hedge gap ahead. Turn left, then quickly right, and follow the path, which runs beside a high flint and gravel wall on the left. In the next corner bear right and continue past the rear of a house and shortly meet a track going left and right. Turn left, go down the track and turn left again when you reach the Haverhill road. A few paces further on turn right into the Ashen Road.

☺ Just after crossing a road bridge, look ahead and find a sign, which indicates you are almost in another county.

Q5 What is the name of the county ahead?

Score 2 points.

⇨ Turn left by a signpost pointing to Clare Castle Country Park and walk by the river back to the car park.

Now add up your score.

More than 28   You're the tops!

20 – 28   You're learning quickly.

Under 20   Better luck next time.

Walk 4. East Bergholt

This interesting walk follows in the footsteps of one of England's most famous landscape painters, John Constable. Starting from the village of East Bergholt where Constable was born, the walk continues to the hamlet of Flatford. In a scene little changed since Constable's day you can wander through lush water meadows bounded by the River Stour. You can also visit the locations where Constable painted many of his masterpieces, including the famous Haywain. There are opportunities to picnic here, feed the ducks or explore the river on foot or by boat. Bridge Cottage, owned by the National Trust, contains a permanent Constable exhibition as well as a teashop and a restored dry dock nearby. A short detour takes you to Flatford Mill once owned by Constable's father. After a short period working at the mill, John followed his boyhood dreams to become a painter and left to attend the R A school. His heart and mind, however, was still exploring the landscape around Flatford and Dedham, where he formerly attended the local grammar school. Writing in 1821, Constable acknowledged how the beauty of the area had inspired his career as a painter. "I associate my 'careless boyhood' with all that lies on the banks of the Stour. They made me a painter, and I am grateful, that is, I had often thought of pictures of them before I had ever touched a pencil." The return route features some more superb views of the Stour Valley, an area designated as being of outstanding natural beauty.

Starting Point: East Bergholt, which lies 8 miles SW of Ipswich. Take the A12 or A137 and then the B1070 road to the village centre.

Parking: Free car park beside Red Lion pub in East Bergholt. Grid Reference: 069 346.

Distance: 3 miles.

Map: OS Explorer No 196 Sudbury, Hadleigh & Dedham Vale.

Terrain: Easy walking mostly along grassy paths with one or two up and downhill stretches.

Pushchairs: Suitable only for use on surfaced paths and roads around East Bergholt and Flatford.

Public Toilets: Car park in East Bergholt and visitor centre at Flatford.

Refreshments: Red Lion pub has a garden and welcomes children. Light refreshments can be obtained from Bridge Cottage tea-room at Flatford. Tel: 01206 298260 for opening times.

Checklist: score 2 points for each

1. A village sign
2. A house named 'Five Firs'
3. A sundial   ·
4. A wooden bridge
5. Some willow trees
6. Boat on the river
7. Some mallard ducks
8. A National Trust sign
9. A small red post-box – near a refreshment kiosk
10. A birds feather
11. A metal stile
12. A kestrel

Total Score _____

The Walk

⇨   Come out of the car park entrance and turn right onto a paved area beside the main road. Look left across the road for an old fashioned sign positioned on a cottage wall.

Q1 According to the sign, what are the items for sale?

Score 2 points.

⇨   Follow the road past the Post Office and to the village sign. Cross the road with care opposite some metal railings at East Bergholt House. This is your first connection with John Constable.

☺   Look for a small plaque attached to the railings.

Q2 In which year was Constable born?

Score 2 points.

⇨   Carry on and enter the churchyard just ahead to have a look at something unusual. It's said that Cardinal Wolsey, Henry VIII's chancellor, financed the tower on St Mary's church but he died too soon and no one has ever completed the work. As you will see, the bells intended for

Bell cage, East Bergholt church

the tower are housed in a 400-year-old wooden bell cage. The bells are mounted on the ground and are rung without ropes. Leave the church-yard and have a look at the front of the church beside the road. Above the porch is a sundial. You'll have to judge for yourself whether the sundial works, assuming it's a sunny day.

Q3 What according to the writing on the sundial "passeth away like a shadow?"

Score 2 points.

⇨   Turn right by the war memorial and proceed down the road by a one way traffic sign. After about 150 metres turn right and go down Fen Lane. Keep following the latter which curves left by a cottage at the bottom. Continue ahead and shortly bear right to cross over a wide cart bridge with metal handrails. Go through a kissing gate and cross Fen Bridge.

☺   Because of access problems, the bridge originally had to be lifted into place by helicopter. Follow the course of the River Stour on your left, as it meanders through some meadows to Flatford Bridge.

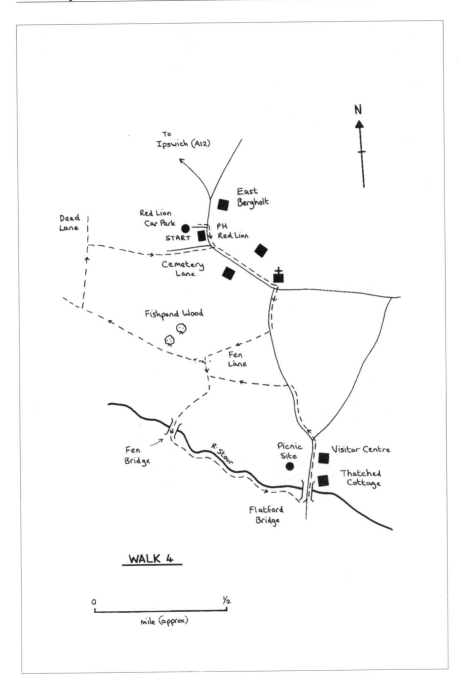

N

To
Ipswich (A12)

East
Bergholt

Dead
Lane

Red Lion
Car Park

START

PH
Red Lion

Cemetery
Lane

Fishpond Wood

Fen
Lane

Fen
Bridge

R. Stour

Picnic
Site

Visitor Centre

Thatched
Cottage

Flatford
Bridge

WALK 4

0   ½

mile (approx)

☺   You might be able to identify some swans, ducks, coots and moorhens which frequent the river here. Before crossing the bridge, you may like to carry on by the river and have a look across the water at Flatford Mill and Willy Lott's cottage, a spot hereabouts where Constable painted his famous Haywain picture. Don't say you've never heard of it!

➩   Retrace your steps back and cross the bridge to arrive beside Bridge Cottage.

Q4   Whose work is permanently featured inside Bridge Cottage? If you haven't guessed already, look to the front of the cottage.

Score 2 points.

➩   Bear left and carry on up the road to reach the visitor centre and toilet block on the right. Look left, go up some steps and continue on a path which leads to a landscaped car park. Carry on through the car park, keeping to the right-hand side. Go through the car park entrance and fork left down a one way road. Continue down a hill to where it bears left at the bottom. Find an entrance on the right, bear left and continue on a path which runs beside a hedge, keeping parallel with the road. Go over a driveway and finally reach a metal stile at the top. Turn left, go over the stile and cross the road. Go over another metal stile in front of you to enter a large field of pasture.

☺   Pause here to admire the sweeping views towards and across the Stour Valley, a scene often sketched and painted by artists from near and far. Would you like to sketch or paint the scene in front?

➩   Carry on down to the bottom of the sloping pasture, veering slightly right and then left to reach and cross a metal stile. Turn right into Fen Lane and follow the latter where it curves right beside a cottage. If you want to take a short cut, continue up the lane and turn left at the top. Otherwise, go left over a stile into some pasture and then shortly over another stile to proceed along a field-edge path with a hedge on the left. Go over another stile and continue with a hedge and fence on the right to the field corner. Cross a stile over a small stream, turn right and then left after 20 metres. Continue ahead and take the next turning right and climb up a leafy lane.

☺   Turn right at the top and continue on a field-edge path. Pause here for a moment and look at the landscape behind you.

Q5 How many churches can you see looking across the valley?

Score 2 points.

⇨   Carry on down the left-hand side of a field and turn right at the bottom. Go over a bridge and a stile to climb up a grassy path and veer right to join Cemetery Lane.

☺   Now for your last question. Look for a plaque on a blue and white building at the top of the lane.

Q6 The plaque marks Constable's studio of _____ ?

Score 2 points.

⇨   Turn left by the Post Office and the car park is just ahead.

Now add up your score.

More than 28   Absolutely brilliant!

20 – 28   Not quite so good!

Under 20   Keep looking!

Walk 5. Eye

The small town of Eye must surely have one of the most unusual and shortest names in the whole of the country. The name is derived from the Saxon word for island. In those days Eye was surrounded by marsh and water and could only be reached by boat. However, during the Norman period the main settlement was situated on high ground; a castle occupied one end and a long bailey stretched westward. The town was built around this outline, which is retained today. To see the outline you can climb some steps up the castle ruins and get a bird's eye view of the town and the surrounding countryside. The nearby 100 ft (33 metre) church tower of St Peter and St Paul was completed in 1470 and has been described as "one of the wonders of Suffolk." The building with the exposed half timbers standing next to the church is the late 15th-century Guildhall, which was once used as a grammar school.

This short walk initially skirts part of the town – still regarded by some as being an antiquated and old fashioned and arguably all the better for it – before entering a pleasant area of woodland. Later, the route crosses some water meadows and the River Dove. From Park Lane, there are grand views of the distant church tower and a wetland habitat, where a pair of binoculars might be handy to watch many of the wildfowl that feed there.

Starting Point: Eye is 13 miles NE of Stowmarket on the B1117 and about 4 miles from Diss on the Norfolk border.

Parking: Cross Street car park in Eye.

Distance: 2.5 miles.

Map: OS Pathfinder No 964 Diss (South) and Botesdale.

Terrain: Metalled Roads, soft earth in woodland and grassy paths.

Pushchairs: Limited to town centre and Town Moor areas.

Public Toilets: Beside the car park in Cross Street.

Refreshments: Beards tea-rooms in Church Street provide a good selection of light refreshments. The Queen's Head pub has a small garden and welcomes children. If you wish, you can take your own food to The Pennings picnic site.

Checklist: score 2 points for each

1. A war memorial
2. Floodlights on a pole
3. A mole hill
4. Nest boxes on a tree trunk
5. A willow tree
6. Mid Suffolk Footpath sign
7. A heron – if you're lucky!
8. Canada geese
9. Signpost stating that Eye is twinned with Pouzauges, France
10. A herd of sheep
11. A fisherman
12. A kissing gate

Total Score _____

The Walk

➪ From the car park entrance turn left to pass between the Queen's Head pub and the Victorian town hall. Turn right at the war memorial and go south along Broad Street.

☺ On the right there is an imposing monument to Sir Edward Kerrison, a local benefactor and one-time MP for Eye.

Q1 Have a closer look at the monument. In which year was Sir Edward born and in which year did he die?

Score 2 points.

➪ Continue along the road and turn right into Magdalen Street (road signed B1117 Stowmarket). In about 75 metres, opposite the entrance to Grampian Foods, turn left and drop down to a recreational ground. Pass the Moors Community Centre on the right and proceed across a gravel car park to the entrance of the Town Moor and Memorial Storm Wood. Cross a concrete bridge into the wood. Immediately bear left keeping parallel with overhead power cables along the southern edge of the wood.

Q2 Just after crossing a small sleeper bridge, look to your right.
    What is positioned beside a small pool? Clue – a romantic
    setting!

Score 3 points.

⇨   Continue through the wood and exit at the far corner. Cross a concrete bridge and follow a stream left to Moorhead Causeway.

☺   The frequent references to Moor and causeway provide a clue
    to the times when Eye was isolated from the rest of the
    countryside. Can you imagine the town being cut-off and
    enclosed by water? Look at the OS map and you'll see that
    even today Eye is surrounded by large areas of agricultural
    countryside.

⇨   Turn right on to the road and follow it to reach Moor Farm. Opposite
a cart shed and barn go left over a stile and enter some pastureland. Continue with a hedge on the right and follow it as it curves right. Look for a
footpath on the left, cross a stile and footbridge and carry on across the
meadow. Cross a culvert and enter a second meadow. Cross over the
River Dove and aim for the stile opposite the other side of the meadow.
Go over the stile and turn left into Park Lane. The distant tower of Eye
church will shortly come into view and also the wetland habitat on the left.

☺   Can you identify any birds here? Maybe there are some
    Canada geese, along with mallard ducks, coots and moorhen.
    On the right-hand side of the lane, some oak trees have been
    planted. Near each tree is a small plaque with details of
    planting.

Q3 What date were the trees planted and for what event?

Score 2 points for each answer

⇨   Carry on ahead and cross straight over the B1077 road. Continue
with a hedge on the right, crossing three stiles in the process.

☺   Just before emerging on to Ludgate Causeway, look for a
    small plate in a garden wall belonging to house No 3.

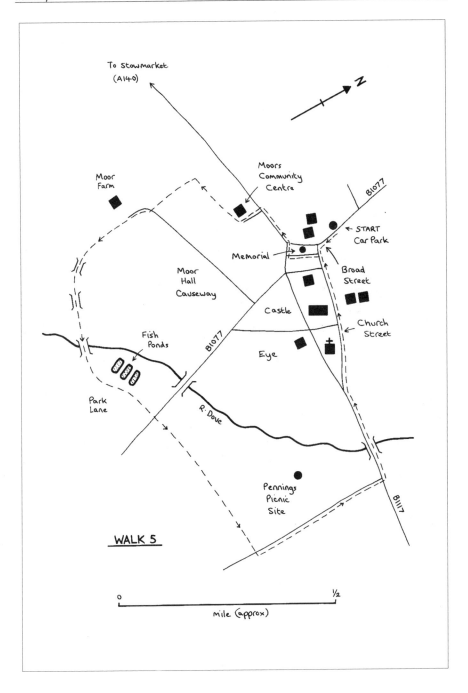

To Stowmarket
(A140)

N

Moors
Community
Centre

B1077

Moor
Farm

← START
Car Park

Memorial

Moor
Hall
Causeway

Broad
Street

Castle

Church
Street

Fish
Ponds

B1077

Eye

Park
Lane

R. Dove

Pennings
Picnic
Site

B1117

WALK 5

0   ½

mile (approx)

Q4 What amount of money was a person liable to pay for not shutting the gate?

Score 2 points.

⇨ Turn left, follow the lane and shortly pass The Pennings picnic site. When you reach the B1117, turn left, cross the Abbey Bridge and walk along the footway. Before the road bends slightly left (take care, visibility is bad here) cross the road and enter the churchyard by a kissing gate. Pass the church on the left and half-timbered Guildhall on the right.

The church and Guildhall

☺ The castle mound is high up in front of you. Proceed along Church Street and keep your eyes open for a road appearing on the right.

Q5 What road shares its name with a famous Duke and soldier?

Score 3 points.

⇨ Continue along Church Street, cross Broad Street and pass the Queen's Head back to your start point.

Well done! Now let's look at the score.

More than 30   Go to the top of the class.

20 – 30   You've got a keen eye.

Under 20   Look a bit harder next time.

Walk 6.
Felixstowe – Landguard Point

With no public footpaths or stiles, and just one kissing gate, this walk is the odd one out. Instead of walking along field-edge paths, we follow sandy embankments and a shingle beach before reaching Landguard Point, the southern-most tip of Suffolk, mouth of the River Orwell and point of entry to the Port of Felixstowe. The quay beside the Orwell is one of immense activity, with giant ship-to-shore cranes loading and offloading containers from all over the world. Elsewhere, mobile gantry cranes move the containers around the port area for onward distribution. You can watch these operations from a viewing area, and observe the large container ships and ferries.

The nearby Landguard Fort, built in 1539 under orders of Henry VIII to protect Harwich harbour, is the fifth fortification built on or near this site. In 1667, the Dutch fleet attacked the fort but the attack was repelled, and so ended the last recorded invasion of English soil. The present fort, built around 1718, had extensive alterations in 1871 and much of the previous structure disappeared. It has recently undergone a further programme of renovation and is now open to the public. For opening times and details of guided tours, contact David Tolliday: 01394 277767. Landguard nature reserve is an important landfall site for migrating birds. Little terns and ringed plovers nest on the bare shingle and their eggs are very well camouflaged. Hence the need to be aware of any area which has been roped off to protect the birds.

Starting Point: Follow the A14 to Felixstowe. Turn off at the first large roundabout signed Felixstowe Docks. Go straight on at the next roundabout, over a railway line and right at the next traffic lights. After 500 metres, where the road bends right, go straight on and turn left. Shortly turn right along Manor Terrace and continue to the car park at the far end.

Parking: Manor Terrace car park. Grid Reference: 290 326.

Distance: 2 miles.

Map: OS Explorer No 197 Ipswich, Felixstowe & Harwich.

Terrain: Steps up and down embankments and an area of shingle beach.

Pushchairs: Suitable only for paths to and from the dock viewing area.

Public Toilets: Some at the car park.

Refreshments: Light refreshments usually available from a van in the dock viewing area. Food outlets on the sea front and in the town centre.

Dockside quay, Felixstowe

Checklist: score 2 points for each

1. An information board
2. A red lifebelt holder
3. Some yachts out to sea
4. A radar scanner mounted on a high column
5. A flashing orange light – on a moving vehicle
6. A rabbit
7. Some bramble bushes
8. Clumps of sea kale – amongst the shingle on the beach
9. Dockside cranes – you can't miss them!
10. Some container boxes – hundreds of them behind the port fence!
11. A wind sock
12. A building clad in silver-blue reflecting glass

Total Score _____

The Walk

⇨ Exit the car park by a notice board listing details of the nature reserve. Follow a gravel path to climb an embankment and reach a higher level. The embankment gives a commanding view of the North Sea. You should see a number of large container ships heading for and leaving Felixstowe port. Shortly go down and up some more steps and carry on along a well-worn path, which runs parallel with the beach. Leave the embankment and eventually enter the Suffolk Wildlife Trust's nature reserve and meet a road coming from your right.

☺ Look for a small information board beside a designated piece of ground.

Q1 What is the name of the rare plant which grows here?

Score 2 points.

⇨ Carry on ahead and pass the Landguard Bird Observatory on the right.

☺   During the bird migratory periods birds are caught here in mist nets. After being weighed and measured (length of the wing) they are ringed and then released.

⇨   At a point where the road bears right to a compound fence, turn left and pass between two half gates. Keep right and head in the direction of the beach and open sea, observing any area roped off to protect nesting birds. Veer right and head towards the water's edge to walk beside the tide line if you wish. The beach is usually deserted here, save for one or two fisherman and walkers.

☺   **For a bonus 3 points** look left and try to discover the outline of Sealand, a wartime fort consisting of two towers joined by a steel platform and positioned some 6 miles out to sea. You'll need keen eyes for this one!

⇨   When you reach the derelict jetty in front, turn right up the beach and walk beside a chainlink fence. At the corner of the fence, follow it round to the left, passing some concrete blocks on the right. Cross a concrete road leading to a gate on the left and pass a red brick house. Keep forward and rejoin a road previously walked. Pass the bird observatory, swing left by the observatory fence and leave the nature reserve by a kissing gate.

☺   On your left now is the large structure of Landguard Fort.

Q2 From which year does the present fort date? Clue – the answer is in the text.

Score 2 points.

⇨   Leave the fort and continue the short distance towards the port viewing area in front of you.

Q3 Look up to one of the giant blue-coloured lifting cranes on the right. What three words are painted on the side?

Score 2 points.

☺   The viewing area allows you to watch at close quarters some of the large (and small) vessels entering and leaving the ports of Felixstowe and Harwich. Near the water's edge is a large information board listing interesting details about the area. From details on the board, find the answer to the following question.

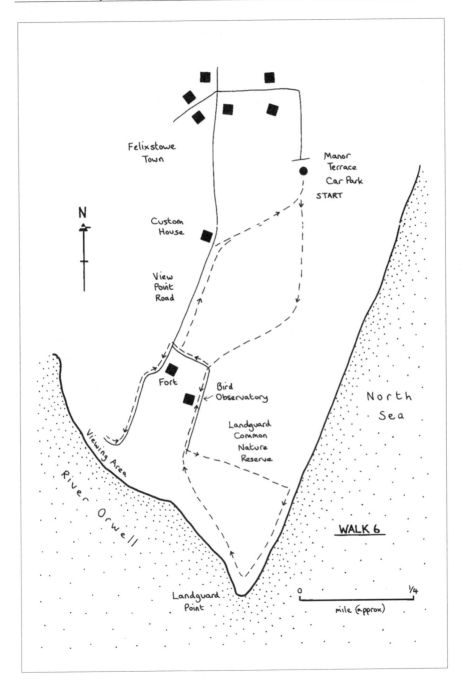

Felixstowe
Town

Manor
Terrace
Car Park
START

N

Custom
House

View
Point
Road

Fort

Bird
Observatory

Landguard
Common
Nature
Reserve

North
Sea

Viewing Area

River Orwell

WALK 6

Landguard
Point

0 ¼

mile (approx)

Q4 How many shipping lines use the port?

Score 2 points.

⇨ Leave the viewing area, retrace your footsteps back to the nature reserve, go through a kissing gate and after 10 metres, turn left to follow a metal fence. Veer to the left of some embankment steps and continue on a narrow road, which soon runs parallel with the dock viewing road. As you approach some caravans bear right and you will see the car park just ahead.

Now add up your score. Did you score the three bonus points?

More than 30   You're unbeatable!

20 – 30   Nearly there!

Less than 20   I don't believe it!

Walk 7. Gazeley, Dalham & Moulton

Youngsters will need plenty of energy and concentration to complete this absorbing walk. The route, known locally as the Three Churches Walk, visits the adjoining villages of Gazeley, Dalham and Moulton, situated near the Suffolk-Cambridgeshire border and the horseracing town of Newmarket. At various points, the walk follows part of the long-distance Icknield Way, which claims to be the oldest road in Britain, dating back to Neolithic times. Elsewhere, a combination of road, woodland and grassy paths, take you to places where there are plenty of interesting things to discover. In the pretty postcard village of Dalham there is an unusual conical malt kiln. Standing not far from Maltings Farm, the kiln was probably used at one time in the local malting trade, long before the industry was modernised. Another attraction is the 15th-century packhorse bridge at Moulton. The bridge, nowadays maintained by English Heritage, was formerly used on the Cambridge to Bury St Edmunds packhorse route. Steps were later added across the road way to deter high-spirited Cambridge under-graduates from crossing the bridge with their motorbikes! Towards the end of the walk, you go past Gazeley stud farm. Youngsters who adore horses will not be disappointed. Usually there are young foals and mares around, which can be seen at fairly close quarters, grazing in paddocks not far from the path. The walk is well waymarked and can be shortened about halfway round if required.

Starting Point: The village of Gazeley is about 5 miles east of Newmarket and is signposted off the A14 from Bury St Edmunds. Take the turn off for Higham and follow the signposts. The walk could also be joined at either Dalham or Moulton.

Parking: Near the Chequers public house. Please park with care and consideration. Grid Reference: 720 642.

Distance: 6.5 or 4.5 miles.

Map: OS Explorer No 210 Newmarket & Haverhill.

Terrain: Good paths with some up and downhill sections.

Pushchairs: Not suitable.

Public Toilets: None on route.

Refreshments: Public houses – the Chequers at Gazeley, Affleck Arms at Dalham (just off route) and Kings Head at Moulton which welcomes children and has a small garden.

Checklist: score 2 points for each

1. Some small columbine flowers
2. A wire fence
3. A pheasant or partridge
4. Some wood chippings
5. A sawn off tree trunk
6. A dandelion flower
7. A four-finger footpath sign
8. A drinking trough in a meadow
9. A magpie
10. A water tower with some aerials on top
11. Some horse stables
12. A tombstone in a churchyard

Total Score _____

The Walk

☺ Before starting, look at the Gazeley village sign on the grass nearby.

Q1 How many horses are on the sign and what is the colour of the horse pulling the plough?

Score 2 points for each answer.

⇨ Cross the main road and take the Higham Road. After about 30 metres turn right towards house No's 1-21 at Tithe Close. Continue on a tarmac path and bear right at number 22. Aim for an alleyway running between two brick walls which leads to a field entrance. Veer left towards an electricity pole in front and shortly continue on a grassy path, which runs parallel with some power cables on the right. Cross into another field with a hedge on the right. Continue ahead, enter another field over a foot-bridge and after 10 metres turn right to enter Bluebutton Wood. Follow the signed route, which goes in and out of the wood. Carry on the same through Blocksey and Brick Kiln Woods, always keeping to the left-hand side and looking for the yellow arrows on marker posts positioned at reg-ular intervals.

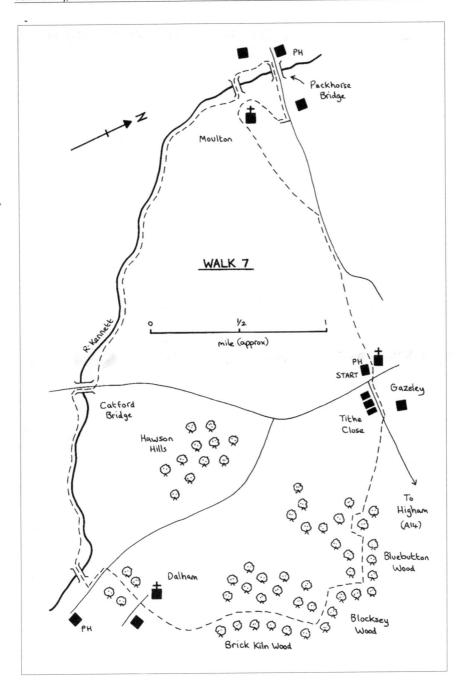

PH

Packhorse Bridge

↑Z

Moulton

WALK 7

0   ½   1
mile (approx)

R. Kennett

PH
START

Gazeley

Catford Bridge

Tithe Close

Hawson Hills

To Higham (A14)

Bluebutton Wood

Dalham

Blocksey Wood

PH

Brick Kiln Wood

☺   Some posts carry a badge denoting that you are on part of the Icknield Way.

Q2   Take a close look at one of the badges. What is the distinctive symbol of the Icknield Way?

Score 2 points.

⇨   Finally exit Brick Kiln Wood, turn right and continue initially on a downhill path by a field-edge, skirting the wood on the right. When you reach the field corner, briefly re-enter the wood, bear left and continue straight ahead to meet a minor road. Turn right here and make your way to St Mary's church at Dalham. Turn left over a strip of grass and pass through a kissing gate. Proceed down through a lovely avenue of mostly chestnut trees.

Q3   About halfway down the avenue what object surrounds a tree trunk?

Score 2 points.

⇨   At the end of the avenue, go through a kissing gate and look for an old wooden notice board beside the hedge.

Q4   What according to the board is the width of the path which walkers should use?

Score 2 points.

⇨   Turn left and continue along the road passing an unusual malt kiln with a tapering red brick structure and a conical roof on the right. After about 35 metres turn right and cross the white footbridge. (The Affleck

Malt kiln

Arms public house is further along the road.) Turn right onto a field-edge path and follow the course of the River Kennett.

☺   Just as you enter another field – after about 200 metres – look to the rear of your left shoulder.

Q5   What kind of building can you just about see over the fields? Clue – it needed plenty of wind!

Score 2 points.

⇨   Continue ahead and turn right when you eventually meet a road. Go over Catford Bridge and take the next left turn to join a bridleway. If you wish to take a short cut, continue up the road to Gazeley village. Otherwise, stay on the bridleway and later a field-edge path until you reach St Peter's church at Moulton.

Q6   Take a look at the church tower. What is "perched" on top of the weather vane?

Score 2 points.

⇨   Turn left over a bridge and then right onto a path with the river beside you on the opposite side. Follow the path to Moulton village and the packhorse bridge. Turn left here if you wish to visit the Kings Head.

Q7   Have a good look at the bridge. How many arches does it have?

Score 2 points.

⇨   Follow the Moulton Road to a pumping station on the left and then turn right. Proceed along a concrete drive and later a grassy path to the rear of the church. Turn left and climb a rising path through some trees and cross a stile to enter a field. Veer slightly right and about halfway up the sloping field, pause and look left.

☺   For 2 bonus points see if you can find the faint outline of Ely Cathedral, a considerable distance away.

⇨   Cross another stile and follow a cross-field path, which leads to a hedge on the left. Go down some steps and turn right onto the road. Carry on along the road and, where it eventually curves left, turn sharp right onto a descending path to reach All Saints Church. Go through the churchyard, turn right and you are back at the start point.

Well done! That really was a long walk. Now have a look at your score.

More than 32   A super effort!

20 – 32   A good score!

Under 20   Try a shorter walk!

Extra congratulations if you scored the bonus!

Walk 8. Hadleigh

Lying at the bottom of a steep-ish valley, it's little wonder that the historic town of Hadleigh is often referred to as "Hadleigh Hole." The wool trade generated the town's initial prosperity. During the 19th and 20th centuries, it became an established centre for milling and malting for the local corn and farming industries. Three important buildings, St Mary's Church, the Deanery Tower and Guildhall stand close together near the town centre and await further discovery. Nowadays a bustling High Street, set astride the A1071, continues to provide the community with a variety of goods and services.

For the walker, however, Hadleigh's real gem is a section of former track bed known as the Hadleigh Railway Walk. It's possible to walk to Raydon, some 2.5 miles distant. This walk, however, only covers about a mile of that distance. Later the route skirts the town area before returning to Station road. When the branch line finally closed to goods traffic in 1965, it left a wonderful legacy for walkers and nature lovers. Nature has been allowed to take its course and embankments and cuttings have been left to grow wild, thus providing buried larders for songbirds and cover for small mammals.

Starting Point: Hadleigh lies 10 miles west of Ipswich and can be approached by the A1071.

Parking: Small car park at the top of Station Road, just off the High Street.

Distance: 4 miles.

Map: OS Explorer No 196 Sudbury, Hadleigh and Dedham Vale.

Terrain: Easy walking along a former track bed, cross-field paths and road surface.

Pushchairs: Only along the track bed for about 1 mile, and around the town area.

Public Toilets: Available in town centre.

Refreshments: A good choice of restaurants, pubs and a teashop in Hadleigh High Street.

Checklist: score 2 points for each

1. A public footpath sign
2. A robin
3. A magpie
4. Horses in a field
5. Power cables
6. A five-barred gate
7. A sycamore tree
8. Clumps of bracken
9. A rabbit
10. A large water tower (look left into the distance for this one)
11. A green and white circular footpath sign
12. A war memorial

Total Score _____

The Walk

⇨   From the car park look for a sign pointing to the Hadleigh Railway Walk and continue along a surfaced path.

☺   The original station building, now converted into a residential house, can be seen to the left. Hadleigh at one time had a large number of maltings and these, too, have now been converted into housing.

⇨   Keep going ahead and shortly walk up a slight incline.

☺   On the left is a milepost erected to mark the creation of a national cycle network. Take a close look at the post.

Q1   Who funded the project and how many mileposts are there altogether?

Score 2 points for each answer.

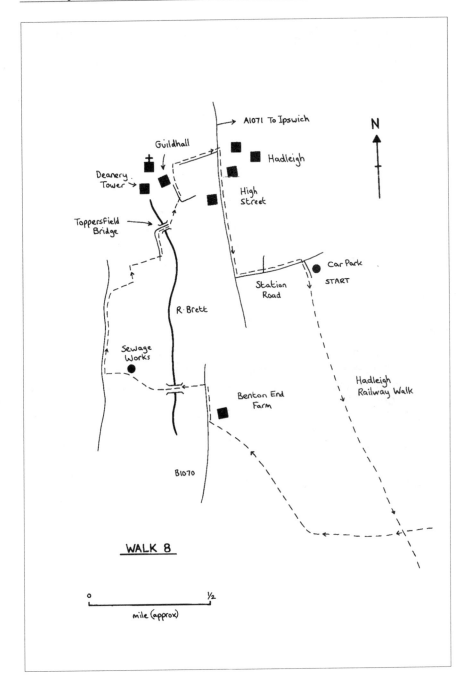

WALK 8

☺ Now you are walking along what was once the railway track bed. The trees and hedgerows either side have been left to grow wild since the branch line closed to traffic. Stroll along the track, close your eyes and it's not too difficult to imagine the line in its heyday. Billowing smoke ... hissing steam ... and a piercing whistle, are a few reminders of the little train, slowly chugging its way back to and from the station at the end of the line.

⇨ Ignore a path going right just before approaching a brick bridge.

☺ The cuttings ahead now get much steeper, especially the one on the left. When the line was constructed before opening in 1847, all the digging was done by hand and the soil removed by horse and cart – no powered earth moving equipment in those days! After a mile, you arrive at a four-way footpath sig.

Q2 Facing straight ahead, where does the left finger on the post point to?

Score 2 points.

⇨ Turn right here and follow a path, which leads to Benton End. Go through a field entrance and continue on a field-edge path. Soon, pass two oak trees on the left and shortly a small copse. The path now bears right and gently rises.

☺ Look to your left for some fine views away over the local countryside. Can you see any sheep or cattle in the meadows?

⇨ At a footpath junction, with a water main on the left, turn right onto a well-defined path which continues to run through an arable field.

⇨ Shortly after passing under some overhead power cables, the path bears left and heads for a spinney in front. The route through the spinney goes up and down with a pylon appearing on the right.

☺ Take a closer look at the pylon.

Q3 To whom does the pylon belong?

Score 3 points.

⇨ Exit the spinney down some steps in the bank and cross a field to reach a large horse chestnut tree. Cross the B1070 in front with care and turn right to walk along a paved area. After about 50 metres turn left by a circular walk sign and go over a stile. Cross a bridge over the River Brett, bear right and cross some pasture land and make for a stile in the corner.

☺ Compare the river bridge with the one at Toppesfield, which you will come to in due course, and note the differences between the dates and methods of construction.

⇨ Go over the stile, quickly followed by another stile. Keep going ahead until you reach a minor road. Turn right and proceed along the road for about 400 metres, turning right when you reach another circular walk sign. Shortly turn left and skirt a sports field, then continue over a small surfaced area. Go left up a small bank and continue beside a wire fence and a Scout Hall on the right.

Q4 What is the name of the hall?

Score 2 points.

⇨ Now turn immediately right and go past another sports field.

Q5 What is the name of the club which plays here and what is the sport?

Score 1 point for each correct answer.

⇨ When you emerge onto a surfaced lane turn left and head up towards Toppersfield Bridge. Turn right over the bridge and after about 30 metres, just short of Silk Mill Lane in front, go left through a metal kissing gate to join a short stretch of river path. Shortly the path leaves the river and continues past a large house on the left to

Deanery Tower

emerge into a short-stay car park. Pass Hadleigh Fire Station on the left and just before reaching the Ram public house turn left onto a path which leads to St Mary's Church, Deanery Tower and Guildhall.

Q6 Each of the above buildings was made from a different material i.e. brick, flint and timber. Match the material with individual buildings.

St Mary's Church _____

Deanery Tower _____

Guildhall _____

Score 1 point for each correct answer.

⇨ Carry on along Church Street and turn right into the High Street. After about 200 metres turn left into Station Road. Walk up the hill and return to your start point.

Well done! Now add up your score.

More than 30   Excellent observation!

20 – 30   You haven't missed much

Under 20   Where have you been looking?

Walk 9. Harleston, Shelland and Onehouse

A few minutes drive from the urban area of Stowmarket brings you to three of the many pretty villages which can be found in the Mid-Suffolk area. Starting from the picnic site at Haughley the walk proceeds through the adjoining villages of Harleston, Shelland and Onehouse. The latter name is something of a misnomer since nowadays there are lots of houses in Onehouse – if you see what I mean! Maybe the name went back to former times when Onehouse Hall dominated a few smaller cottages in the village.

There are plenty of things to see and explore on the walk. In Northfield Wood, you can see evidence of the ancient art of coppicing being practised, whereby trees are cut back in order to let more light in and encourage further growth. Sometimes there is someone cutting logs to produce commercial charcoal. The church at Onehouse set amongst some fields is unusual in that it has a round tower, which has been partially rebuilt during recent years. Another unusual feature is the moat around New Farm in Shelland. If you are very, very lucky, you may see some Muntjac deer, which roam the immediate countryside. But beware, they are very shy animals. Once they have spotted you they tend to run away and disappear across the fields into the undergrowth.

Starting Point: Haughley picnic site is 3 miles north of Stowmarket beside the A14. Vehicles approaching from the direction of Bury St Edmunds should cross the dual carriageway with care.

Parking: Ample parking at Haughley picnic site. Grid Reference: 022 617.

Distance: 5.5 miles.

Map: OS Explorer No 211 Bury St Edmunds & Stowmarket.

Terrain: Mostly field-edged paths with some up and down hill stretches. Conditions may be muddy in Northfield Wood so stout footware is advised.

Pushchairs: Not suitable.

Public Toilets: At the picnic site.

Refreshments: Tables available at the picnic site. Otherwise, there are plenty of food and drink outlets in Stowmarket.

Checklist: score 2 points for each

1. A rabbit
2. A dead tree
3. Some bales of hay
4. A butterfly
5. A kissing gate
6. Some wood logs
7. A bird's feather
8. A church spire – not a tower!
9. A farm tractor
10. A skylark
11. A distant television transmitter
12. Some beehives

Total Score _____

The Walk

⇨ Leave the picnic site and turn left on to the Harleston Road.

Q1 Look at the road sign on the left. What should motorists watch out for during the next 2 miles?

Score 2 points.

⇨ Turn right and go up a bank by a public footpath sign. Cross the field (the path may be ill-defined here) and head towards the edge of Broad Border plantation of trees in front. When you reach the woodland, turn left and continue walking parallel with the trees and a ditch on the right. At the field boundary, go past a substantial wooden bridge and enter the next field. Continue ahead to reach, eventually, a roadway leading to White House Farm on the left. Cross straight over the road to enter a field opposite.

⇨ After 20 metres swing left then right and continue on a field-edge path with a hedge on the right. Keep going ahead to enter another field, passing a stagnant pond on the left.

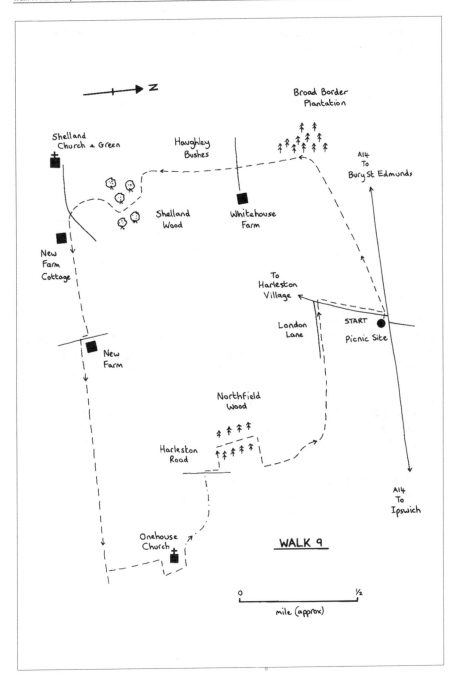

N

Broad Border
Plantation

Shelland
Church & Green

Haughley
Bushes

A14
To
Bury St Edmunds

Shelland
Wood

Whitehouse
Farm

New
Farm
Cottage

To
Harleston
Village

London
Lane

START
Picnic Site

New
Farm

Northfield
Wood

Harleston
Road

A14
To
Ipswich

Onehouse
Church

WALK 9

0 —————————— ½

mile (approx)

Q2 Now look for some electricity cables crossing the field. How many lines are there?

Score 2 points.

⇨ Carry on to an area known as Haughley Bushes and go past a four-finger footpath sign and a substantial farmhouse on the right.

Q3 What is present in a channel just the other side of the hedge? Perhaps the whole building was moated at one time.

Score 2 points.

⇨ Stay on the field-edged path and continue in the direction of Shelland Wood in front. Soon after, the path curves left at the field boundary, carry on with the woodland on the right. Look for and shortly cross a footbridge into the wood. Notice how the short walk through the wood provides a pleasant interlude away from field-edged paths.

⇨ Continue straight ahead for about 30 metres and look for another footbridge on the left. Cross the bridge and turn right. Follow the wood for 20 metres and then turn left to continue with a hedge on the right. Pass an area of scrubland and a pond on the right. Continue to the far end of the field to meet a narrow road. Turn right here and follow the road round to Shelland Green.

Q4 Have a look at the village sign near the church. What animals are depicted on the sign?

Score 2 points.

⇨ Retrace your steps back to where the road curves left, but continue straight ahead to join a grassy path. Pass New Cottage set back on the right and maintain direction to reach a road junction and turn right. After 25 metres, find a narrow path on the left. Turn left onto the path, which runs between the moated New Farm on the left and a bungalow on the right. Bear left, pass some farm buildings and carry on along a grassy path.

☺ Keep your eyes skinned for any deer, which often frequent the surrounding fields.

⇨ Ignore an official path going left and go over a sleeper bridge to shortly enter another field. Do you realise we haven't crossed a stile yet?

Onehouse church

Take the next turning left on to a field-edged path with a ditch on the right and head in the direction of Onehouse church.

⇨ At the field boundary turn right and then left to shortly pass in front of the church. Continue along a track to reach the Harleston Road. Turn right here and proceed to Woodland Close. Turn left and make your way along a surfaced path to Northfield Wood in front. Go through a kissing gate into the wood and then swing right and left onto the main ride. Veer left after 50 metres onto a narrow path, go over a small sleeper bridge and continue through the wood.

Q5 Look around the wood as you pass through and identify some of the trees. Which is the tree most likely to be found in the wood – lemon, ash or cherry?

Score 3 points.

☺ I hope you're not feeling too tired. You've got about another mile or so back to the start.

⇨ Exit the wood, continue along a narrow strip and turn right at the end. Continue beside a hedge thicket. Where the latter ends turn left onto a cross-field path. The path runs uphill and veers right to the field edge. Carry on for another 150 metres to reach a footpath sign beside a tree and turn left. Go straight ahead and cross a field to join London Lane in front.

☺   If you haven't found the beehives on the checklist, look to your right about now! Turn right at the end of the lane and proceed along the road to reach the picnic site. Just before reaching the site, look up at an overhead barrier.

Q6 What is the permitted height for vehicles entering the site?

Score 2 points.

If you saw any deer along the walk, add an extra **3 bonus points**.

Well done. Now add up your score.

More than 34   Super stuff!

25 – 34   Not bad!

Under 25   Was it that difficult?

Walk 10. Hoxne

*The large village of Hoxne –pronounced 'Hoxon' – lies near the
Norfolk border and is bounded by the Rivers Waveney and Dove. Over
the centuries, Hoxne has been associated with the legend of King
Edmund. Born in Saxony in 841, Edmund was crowned King of the
East Angles whilst still a teenager and went on to become patron saint
of England. The legend has it that, after fighting a bloody battle,
Edmund hid under the Goldbrook Bridge before being spotted by a
newly wed couple. They saw the reflection of his spurs in the water
and betrayed his hiding place to the Danes. Edmund supposedly put a
curse on all newly weds crossing the bridge and, to this day, some
brides take care to avoid it. After his death in 870, Edmund's body was
enshrined at Boedericsworth, which would later become the town of
Bury St Edmunds. There are some references to this ancient King and
martyr on the walk waiting for you to discover. The village hall contains
some relief sculptures of the St Edmund legend, which can be found
on one of the walls. Elsewhere Hoxne has some picturesque cottages
standing around the village green. The church of St Peter and St Paul
is a large structure standing on high ground above the village and
contains some wall paintings and a local history display. Field-edge
paths take you to Cross Street, a scattered settlement about half a
mile away from the village centre. The walk also covers a short stretch
beside the Goldbrook, a small stream.*

Starting Point: Hoxne village is about 4 miles NE of Eye on the B1118.

Parking: Hoxne village hall, just over the Goldbrook bridge. Grid
Reference: 180 769.

Distance: 3.5 miles.

Map: OS Explorer No 230 Diss & Harleston.

Terrain: Mostly field-edge and cross-field paths with some stretches of
road walking.

Pushchairs: Suitable only on surfaced roads in Hoxne village.

Public Toilets: None on route.

Refreshments: The Swan public house has riverside gardens and
welcomes children. Light refreshments are available from the Post Office
stores in Hoxne and a shop in Cross Street.

Checklist: score 2 points for each

1. Some horse chestnut trees
2. The name 'Kingswood' on a barred gate
3. A red telephone box
4. A wooden shelter
5. An ash tree
6. A sleeper bridge
7. A plantation of young saplings
8. A junior horse equestrian event course
9. A thatched barn
10. A pigeon
11. A house named 'Parkside'
12. A tall conifer hedge

Total Score _____

The village green, Hoxne

The Walk

▷   Leave the car park and turn left, go over the Goldbrook bridge to reach a road junction. Turn right, walk along a paved area over the River Dove, and pass the Swan public house. Fork right by a telephone box, pass the village green on the left and continue up Low Street to join the Stradbroke Road opposite the church.

☺   On the other side of the road are some almshouses.

Q1   Look closely at the first house. What date can you see on a brick inscribed Oakley Terrace?

Score 2 points.

▷   Turn right and proceed along the Stradbroke Road and go past Church Close.

☺   The area near the entrance to Watermill Lane was formerly known as Nine Oaks corner. Nowadays, however, fewer trees exist.

Q2   How many trees are there on the triangular piece of ground in front of you?

Score 3 points.

▷   Continue ahead for about 100 metres and just after passing Mulberry Cottage, turn right by a footpath sign and carry on with a hedge on the left. Follow the path as it shortly curves right and pass a barn on the left. The grassy path now runs between an arable field and a plantation of young trees to reach a footpath junction. If you want to take a short cut, turn right and head back towards the Swan public house.

▷   Otherwise, turn left down a slope and carry on to shortly cross a bridge at the bottom. Pass a three-finger footpath sign and continue for 20 metres to reach another one. Bear left, go over an access driveway and go left of the hedge in front. However, if the path is overgrown, go to the right of the hedge as the locals appear to do. You should shortly arrive at a water treatment works.

☺   Some of these treatment works nowadays employ high-tech equipment as you can see.

Q3 What object is sited under a small wind turbine?

Score 2 points.

⇨ Go left over a sleeper bridge and turn right onto a field-edge path.

☺ As you proceed ahead look to an adjoining field on your right. A stone memorial to St Edmund stands in this field. You can get a close up view by taking a permissive path. Score 3 bonus points if you spot it.

⇨ You can get a close up view by taking a permissive path. Keep straight ahead and follow a succession of field-edge paths for about 600 metres, ignoring paths going left and right, to arrive by a garage and shop at Cross Street. Turn left into Cross Street and soon arrive at a well, now a bus shelter.

Q4 Look upwards here. What item stands above some unusual metal road signs?

Score 2 points.

⇨ Turn right and proceed along Nuttery Vale road. After 150 metres turn right beside a footpath sign and join a grassy path. Go over a stile and cross a sleeper bridge over a ditch. Turn left and follow the path to the field corner where it curves right. Go left over a ditch here and enter another field. Continue down the sloping field with a hedge on the left.

⇨ At the bottom of the field go over a stile and turn right. After walking parallel with the Goldbrook for 20 metres, turn left, cross over a wooden bridge and go through a gate at the far end into a field. Go straight ahead on a cross-field path to reach the road at the far end. Turn right here, proceed down the road and go past Fairstead Farm and another building.

Q5 What is the missing word which completes the name of this building? The Old _____ House.

Score 2 points.

It was around this area in November 1992 that the greatest Roman treasure ever to be discovered in this country was unearthed. The treasure, consisting of some 14,000 coins and 200 objects all of gold and silver, was dug up by a local man who was searching with a metal detector for a friend's hammer. A lucky find indeed!

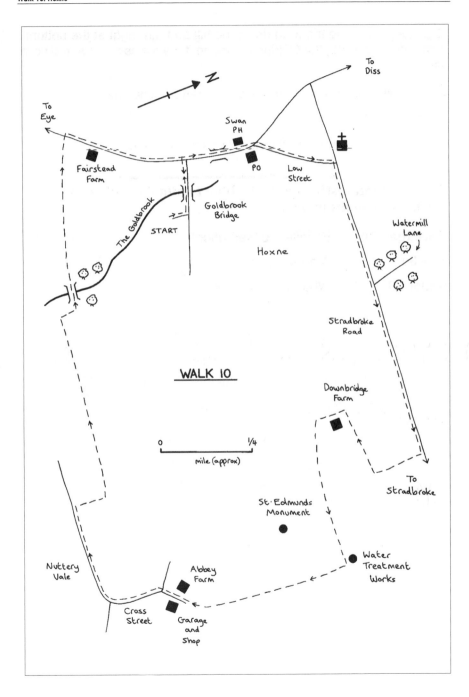

WALK 10

To Eye

To Diss

Swan PH

Fairstead Farm

PO

Low Street

Goldbrook Bridge

START

The Goldbrook

Hoxne

Watermill Lane

Stradbroke Road

Downbridge Farm

St. Edmunds Monument

Water Treatment Works

To Stradbroke

Nuttery Vale

Abbey Farm

Cross Street

Garage and Shop

0   ¼
mile (approx)

⇨   Keep following the road down the hill and turn right at the bottom. Just before crossing the Goldbrook bridge, take a close look at the right pillar.

Q6 On what date was King Edmund taken prisoner here?

Score 2 points.

⇨   Go over the bridge and turn right back into the car park.

After that interesting walk, it's time to add up your score. Did you get the bonus points?

More than 30   Excellent observation!

20 – 30   A good score!

Under 20   What did you miss?

Walk 11. Lavenham

It is hard to believe nowadays perhaps, but in Medieval times Lavenham was reckoned to be the fourteenth wealthiest town in England. The town grew rich from the manufacture of woollen cloth during the 14th to16th centuries. With its splendid Church and many fine timber-framed houses, Lavenham is regarded as being the finest surviving example of a Medieval town. In Church Street and the busy High Street the houses intermingle with small cottages, some of which lean and hang together at crazy angles. The author of the old nursery rhyme "There was a crooked man, who lived in a crooked house etc" would have been at home in Lavenham! Talking of writers, did you know that Jane Taylor who wrote the verse "Twinkle, twinkle little star," lived in nearby Shilling Street?

The Medieval street pattern still exists, complete with the market place, dominated by the historic Guildhall. The building is open to the public and includes a history of the local cloth trade. A railway line, which once served the town, has since been dismantled and now forms part of this pleasant walk. Strictly speaking, the path is not a public right of way but a route managed by Suffolk County Council for walkers and riders. After a tour through the town, the walk circles the immediate countryside, which is dominated by the 141ft (43 metres) church tower of St Peter and St Paul.

Starting Point: Lavenham is on the A1141, about 10 miles south of Bury St Edmunds. It is also signposted from the B1115.

Parking: Free car park in Church Street. Grid Reference: 913 496.

Distance: 3 miles.

Map: OS Explorer No 196 Sudbury, Hadleigh & Dedham Vale.

Terrain: Easy walking along surfaced roads and a dismantled railway track which can be sticky underneath in places.

Pushchairs: Suitable only in the town area, and railway walk (if dry).

Public Toilets: At the car park.

Refreshments: The Cock public house beside the car park has a small garden and welcomes children. Tea-rooms can be found in the Guildhall and along the High Street.

Checklist: score 2 points for each

1. A red telephone box
2. TT 1856 – on a house towards the far end of the High Street
3. A brick bridge
4. A builders yard
5. An ash tree
6. A stile with a footrest
7. Imprint of horse's hooves
8. Some exposed tree roots
9. A church tower seen from a distance
10. An oak tree
11. Some chickens
12. A willow tree hanging over a small pond

Total Score _____

Lavenham

The Walk

⇨ Leave the car park and turn right into Church Street and admire the timber-framed houses. Go past the Swan Hotel and up the High Street.

☺ Keep looking for the odd shaped house, including a small crooked one on the left.

⇨ When you reach Market Lane turn right and make a short detour to the market place.

Q1 What is the name of the magnificent timber-framed building on the right?

Score 2 points.

⇨ Retrace your steps back to the High Street and turn right. Continue towards the end of the High Street to a point where the road curves left, just before a brick bridge. Cross the road with care and take a path by a board welcoming you to the Lavenham Walk. Follow the path round to join the route of the former track bed of the Long Melford to Bury St Edmunds branch line, which runs straight and level with vegetation either side.

☺ The line, which was opened by the Great Eastern Railway Company in August 1865, was active for almost 100 years before its final closure in April 1965.

⇨ Carry on along a well-worn path, which can be boggy in places, especially after spells of inclement weather. Ignore paths going left and right to arrive at Park Road. Walk up the slope, go through the gates, across the road and down the other side to rejoin the track bed.

☺ Shortly you will see a wooden seat on the right-hand side.

Q2 What are the initial letters carved on the back of the seat?

Score 2 points.

⇨ Maintain direction between noticeably raised embankments with tall overhanging trees giving a lovely tunnel effect.

☺ In days of steam, the vegetation would have been cut well back, in case a spark from the engine set the whole countryside alight!

⇨ Go under a brick bridge, bear right up a sloping path and turn right at the top to join Bridge Street Road. Follow the road over the bridge and continue ahead to reach a farm.

Q3 Look high and to the right. What is the name of the farm formed by letters hanging in a semi-circle over the farm entrance?

Score 2 points.

⇨ Carry on along the road for about another 400 metres and turn left when you reach a circular walk sign to enter a field. Continue on a broad path, heading towards the imposing sight of Lavenham church tower.

Q4 How high do you think the tower is? Clue – the answer is in the text.

Score 2 points.

⇨ Look right soon for a cricket pitch and a pavilion with the letters LCC on the front.

Q5 What do you think LCC represents?

Score 3 points.

⇨ Go through two gateways with stiles and turn right when you reach Potland Lane. Head towards the church and turn left up some steps at the foot of the church tower. Turn right and follow the path around the church leading out into Church Street. Turn left, cross the road by the Cock Inn and return back to the car park.

Well done. Now add your score.

More than 30   Quite outstanding!

20 – 30   Pretty good try!

Under 20   Well, never mind!

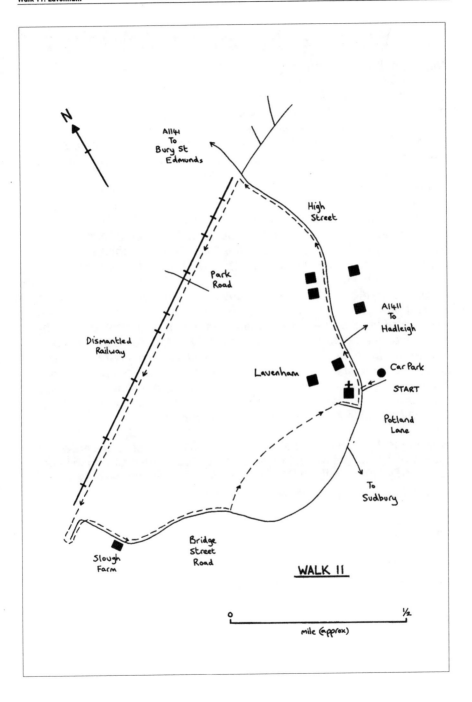

N

A1141
To
Bury St
Edmunds

High
Street

Park
Road

A1411
To
Hadleigh

Dismantled
Railway

Lavenham

Car Park

START

Potland
Lane

To
Sudbury

Slough
Farm

Bridge
Street
Road

WALK 11

0   ½
mile (approx)

Walk 12. Needham Market

Needham Lake is a former gravel pit from where minerals were extracted to help build the nearby A14 road. When extraction was completed the pit was flooded and it is now used for recreational purposes, drawing hundreds of visitors, especially during the spring and summer months. Besides having a level surface around the perimeter, good for wheel and pushchair access, the lake caters for fishermen and model boat enthusiasts. It is a haven for wildlife, particularly birds. Gulls, coot, swans and Canada geese are regular visitors and, during summertime, swallows skim the surface looking for insects. Elsewhere, by the bankside, geese and ducks eagerly await crusts of bread from excited youngsters. In the middle of the lake, a wind-operated aerator keeps the water fresh and free of algae. Running in part beside the lake is the River Gipping, once a commercial waterway linking Ipswich and Stowmarket, a distance of some 17 miles. The river was canalised in 1793 and soon horse-drawn barges, carrying slate, coal and manure were a common sight. After skirting one side of the lake, the walk continues through a small nature reserve, along the river towpath and past some water meadows. The return journey includes Needham's High Street, which contains some interesting buildings, including a church with a magnificent hammer beam roof and later some old almshouses. Station Yard has a Grade II listed railway station opened in 1849. Nearby is a narrow tunnel, which runs under the railway. Youngsters will be able to stand upright here but adults, however, will have to bend their backs.

Starting Point: Needham Lake, beside the B1078, a short distance from the town centre. Ignore the tarmac entrance, continue over a road bridge and shortly turn left off the B1078 by a sign indicating the lake car park.

Parking: Ample parking at Needham Lake. Grid Reference: 094 546.

Distance: 2.5 miles.

Map: OS Explorer No 211 Bury St Edmunds & Stowmarket.

Terrain: Easy walking mainly on surfaced paths but stout footwear advised for the towpath.

Pushchairs: A hard surfaced footpath surrounds the entire lake.

Public Toilets: At Needham Lake and at Barratts Lane in the High Street.

Refreshments: Light refreshments available at the lake. A varied selection of shops and pubs in Needham High Street.

Checklist: score 2 points for each

1. A swan
2. A lifebelt holder
3. A seagull
4. A brown seat
5. A coot
6. A goalpost
7. A passenger or freight train
8. A model sailing boat
9. A duck
10. A rabbit
11. A fishing rod
12. Some metal railings

Total Score _____

Hawks Mill

The Walk

⇨ Leave the car park and take a surfaced path with a children's' play area on the left. Further over to the left is Bosmere Mill, currently being restored. Go past a Gipping Valley Footpath sign and cross a large wooden bridge over the River Gipping. Turn right and walk with the lake on the left. Stay on a tarmac surface and shortly enter a small nature reserve.

☺ Look for a small sign – there are several of them on the walk.

Q1 What are you asked to take home with you?

Score 2 points.

☺ There are small islands created here amongst the reed beds. Can you see any butterflies or birds here?

⇨ Continue to a point where the path bears left just before a seat. Turn right on a mown path with long grass on either side. The path shortly runs parallel with a sports field, known locally as the Camping Land. If this path is unclear, simply head towards the railway station ahead and turn right along a well-worn path; otherwise, continue to the far end of the field and take a look at the front of a large wooden hut.

Q2 What is the name of the group that meets here?

Score 2 points.

⇨ Go through a gateway and enter Crown Street with some houses appearing on the right. When you arrive at a bridge with iron railings turn right and cross the River Gipping. Turn left onto a narrow surfaced path and, after about 30 metres, veer left across the grass towards a road bridge.

☺ You may come across some local lads here engaged in a spot of fishing. Be careful not to trip over any bicycles lying around!

⇨ Go under the bridge to join the river path and shortly pass a small weir, which controls the flow of water. After heavy rain, the river often floods the low-lying meadows but along other stretches it is sluggish and shallow.

☺ Soon you will see a sign beside the riverbank.

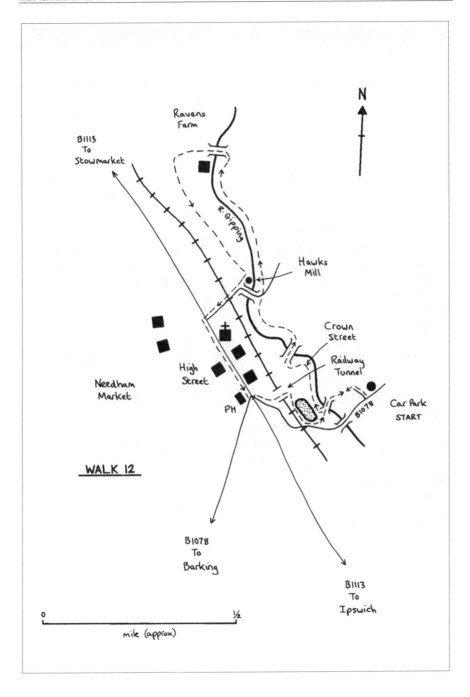

N

Ravens
Farm

B1113
To
Stowmarket

R. Gipping

Hawks
Mill

Crown
Street

Railway
Tunnel

Needham
Market

High
Street

PH

B1078

Car Park
START

WALK 12

B1078
To
Barking

B1113
To
Ipswich

0   ½
mile (approx)

Q3 What activity does the sign say is dangerous here?

Score 2 points.

⇨   Carry on ahead beside the river for another 250 metres and ignore a footpath going right. When you come to the next bridge at Ravens Farm, turn left, cross the bridge and go over a stile. With Ravens Farm on the left, pass some wooden fencing and head towards the railway line in front.

☺   Trains pass here frequently and it may get you points for your checklist. Take the next turning left, go through a kissing gate and walk beside some hay meadows, which contain a mixture of natural grasses and wild flowers.

⇨   Ignore a path going right up some steps towards the railway line and continue on a grassy path. Go through another kissing gate and shortly emerge with some stables on the left. Continue ahead and shortly meet a road junction. Just over the bridge to the left stands the historic building of Hawksmill.

☺   There has been a mill on this site since the Domesday book was compiled. However, the building you see today was built in 1884.

⇨   Turn right, carry on walking up Hawksmill Street and pass under a rail bridge.

Q4 What is the maximum height for vehicles passing under the bridge?

Score 2 points.

⇨   Go up some steps and reach the junction with the B1113. Turn left into Needham High Street and walk along the paved area.

☺   Gaze into the shop windows and discover the variety of goods and services supplied to Needham and the local area. The street has some old buildings on the opposite side of the road, including one just before reaching the church.

Q5 There is a date and two initial letters shown on the house. What are they?

Score 2 points.

☺   It may seem strange to see a church oddly positioned by the side of a busy main street. The church was built in the 15th century and was a chapel of ease to nearby Barking church until 1901, so there is no churchyard. Pop inside the church – if it's open – and admire the double hammer-beamed roof (ask someone to explain this to you!). Outside, look at the noticeboard.

Q6   To which saint is the church dedicated?

Score 2 points.

⇨   Continue walking down the street and when you reach the Swan public house opposite, turn left into Station Yard.

☺   Until the 1950s the yard contained coal wagons, rail sidings and a corn mill. Ahead of you is the railway station designed by Frederick Barnes who was also responsible for the designing the town hall in the main street.

Q7   On which date was the station officially opened? Clue – look for a plaque on the station wall.

Score 2 points.

⇨   Head towards the left of the station. Go downhill and enter a narrow rail tunnel.

☺   You can shout, whistle or sing as loud as you like.!

⇨   Exit, right, from the tunnel and head back towards the lake. Join the tarmac surface again, go past the amenities building on the right and finally back to the car park.

_____

Well done! Now add up your score.

More than 30   Excellent score!

18 – 30   You're getting better!

Under 18   Were you asleep?

Walk 13. Orwell Country Park

The townspeople of Ipswich – and any visitor for that matter – are particularly fortunate to have a country park almost on their doorstep. The Orwell Country Park covers about 150 acres of land, comprising mainly of Bridge Wood and Pipers Vale, which are linked by the sandy foreshore of the River Orwell. You can follow two different walks within the wood, each marked with a colour band. This well-defined walk is coloured red and is known as the Orwell Orbital, a distance of about 3.5 miles with the choice of adding a further half-mile later on. Bridge Wood has plenty of space to move around in, enough for youngsters to let off steam and play hide and seek perhaps. The woodland consists mainly of sycamore, Corsican and Scots pine as well as some English oaks. The wood is also home to a variety of birds and animals. If you are very lucky, you may come across a fox or roe deer, which frequent the area. The walk follows a delightful stretch of the Orwell foreshore. There is always something of interest happening on the river; whether it is the sight of sailing craft, or commercial shipping making its way to and from the inland port of Ipswich. Dominating the local landscape is the Orwell Bridge, which was opened in 1982 and is 1278 metres in length. You can walk underneath this massive concrete engineering feat and marvel at its construction. Here you have the choice of retracing your steps or walking to the top of Pipers Vale. The cliff top path, which gently runs down to the estuary shore, allows excellent views over the water to the Shotley peninsula.

Starting Point: Bridge Wood is situated on the eastern side of Ipswich. Come off the A14 at the Nacton exit, go left round a roundabout and after a further 100 metres turn sharp left onto a signposted road, which leads to the park.

Parking: Ample parking at Bridge Wood car park.

Distance: 3.5 or 4 miles.

Map: OS Explorer No 197 Ipswich, Felixstowe and Harwich.

Terrain: Good paths with some gentle up and downhill sections.

Pushchairs: Limited use on some broad paths within Bridge Wood.

Public Toilets: None on route.

Refreshments: None on walk but a path through the picnic area leads to the Little Chef restaurant and service station shop beside the A14. Picnic tables available at Bridge Wood.

Checklist: score 2 points for each

1. Bird boxes on a tree trunk
2. Some tall pine trees
3. A grey squirrel
4. Square signs coloured red and white – used as orienteering stations
5. Some cones on the floor
6. A caravan park
7. A pigeon
8. A burnt-out tree trunk
9. A robin
10. A wire fence
11. A marker buoy on the river
12. Graffiti on some concrete

Total Score _____

The Walk

☺   Before starting the walk take a look at the large notice board positioned near the start. This gives information on the various routes, wildlife habitats and a brief background to the history of the park etc.

Q1   In which year was the park officially opened to the public?

Score 2 points.

⇨   Go left through a metal gate and follow the path leading into Bridge Wood. Where a path comes in from the left, carry straight on. Look for a short wooden post with a red band and turn left onto a well-used path which skirts the wood on the right. Keep going ahead and pass a caravan site situated behind a fence.

☺   Look right for a gap in the woodland edge and spot some wood sculptures. Take a closer inspection.

Q2 What is the date inscribed on one piece of sculpture?

Score 3 points.

⇨ The path shortly meanders downhill to the right and through a large clearing.

☺ Look to the left and a golf course will shortly appear.

Q3 What is the colour of the triangle at the top of the marker flag?

Score 3 points.

⇨ The River Orwell now gradually comes into view. Go down some steps onto the foreshore straight ahead and

Wood sculptures, Orwell Country Park

turn right. Depending on the tide times, you may well be able to continue walking along the foreshore for some distance. However, it is better to follow a route back through the woodland edge along higher ground, where the bank gives grand views across the river and beyond. Continue along the foreshore for about 20 metres and turn right onto a path which heads back into the wooded area.

☺ When you get to a seat with a lone oak tree in front, look slightly to the left and on the opposite bank you may be able to spot a large brick tower. Freston Tower is in fact a 'folly' – something built to be looked at rather than lived in. Legend has it that the tower was built so the owner's daughter, Ellen De Freston, could study a different subject each day in the six tower rooms. A more likely explanation is that it was once a lookout tower for shipping on the river.

⇨ Carry on ahead along the top of a sandy bank, still following the red banded posts positioned at regular intervals. After passing a wildlife pond, go over a slatted footbridge with a handrail, and look across to the right amongst some vegetation.

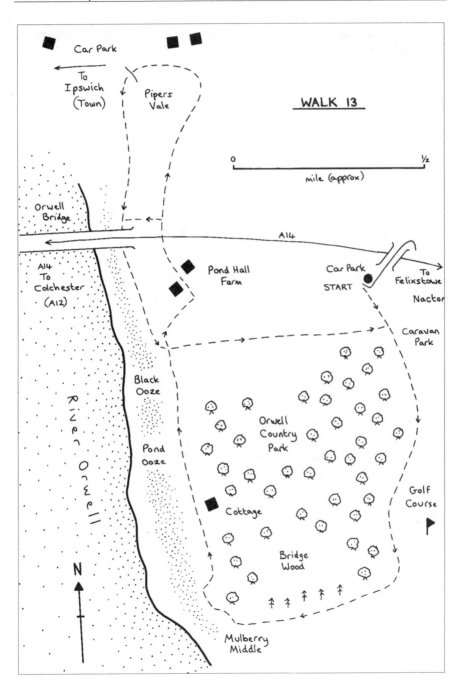

Car Park

To
Ipswich
(Town)

Pipers
Vale

WALK 13

0   ½

mile (approx)

Orwell
Bridge

A14

A14
To
Colchester
(A12)

Pond Hall
Farm

Car Park

START

To
Felixstowe

Nacton

Caravan
Park

Black
Ooze

River Orwell

Pond
Ooze

Orwell
Country
Park

Golf
Course

Cottage

Bridge
Wood

N

Mulberry
Middle

Q4 What is the colour of the partially secluded Downham Reach Cottage?

Score 2 points.

⇨   You will soon leave the wooded area with pasture appearing on the right. Where the pasture boundary ends, turn sharp right and continue on a narrow path, which leads to Pond Hall Farm. Pass some farm buildings either side of the path and head towards the Orwell Bridge. If you want to lengthen the walk by a half mile or so and reach the top of Pipers Vale, carry on straight ahead and shortly turn left off Gainsborough Lane near an old oak tree. Follow the path round, go left through a metal access gate and head down towards the river. Otherwise, turn left, go over a stile and walk parallel with the bridge for about 30 metres.

☺   Pause here for a close-up view of this impressive concrete structure with road traffic passing overhead.

Q5 What is the total length of the bridge? Clue – the answer is in the text.

Score 2 points.

⇨   Pass under the bridge and follow a path which leads down to the foreshore again.

☺   Near the tideline you might be able to spot wading birds searching for worms amongst the squelch and ooze. Further along you may see the odd fisherman with a spade and bucket, digging for bait.

⇨   Turn left and retrace your steps back into the woodland. When you reach a post with a blue band, turn left and stay on a steadily rising path. At the top, turn left and return to your start point.

Now it's time to add up your score.

More than 30   Absolutely brilliant!

20 – 30   You haven't missed much!

Less than 20   Better luck next time.

Walk 14. Pin Mill

Just off the main road at Chelmondiston lies the hamlet of Pin Mill, a popular area for walking and relaxation. The small community here, some live on houseboats moored at the water's edge, is often joined by artists who are attracted by the natural beauty of one of the prettiest parts of the River Orwell. The children's writer, Arthur Ransome, who wrote 'Swallows and Amazons' and 'We Didn't Mean to Go to Sea', once lived here. The origins of the Butt and Oyster public house standing on the waterfront go back to the mid-sixteenth century.

Pin Mill is also favoured by yachtsmen seeking a safe anchorage. Often sharing the river with dinghies and an assortment of other pleasure craft, are some Thames sailing barges. With their characteristic tan sails, they regularly plied their trade along the coast before road transport took over. Later, the walk takes you along sandy paths and through a small wooded area to Woolverstone marina where all types of boats are moored and can be seen undergoing repairs. In centuries past contraband smuggling was rife on the river and the Cat House is a passing reminder of those times. The imposing building of Woolverstone Hall was built in 1776 and is now occupied by the Ipswich School for Girls. Part of the return journey crosses some pastureland and goes along field-edge paths. Through gaps in the hedgerow positioned on high ground, there are tantalising glimpses of the Orwell, where fields and parkland reach down to the water's edge.

Starting Point: The hamlet of Pin Mill is 6 miles south of Ipswich. Take the B1456 turn off at Chelmondiston and follow the road signs.

Parking: Pay and display car park on approach to Pin Mill Grid Reference: 205 379.

Distance: 3 miles.

Map: OS Explorer No 197 Ipswich, Felixstowe & Harwich.

Terrain: Easy walking on good paths.

Pushchairs: Not really suitable.

Public Toilets: Some at Pin Mill.

Refreshments: Butt and Oyster pub welcomes families. Light refreshments including ice cream and soft drinks etc available at Pin Mill shop. Picnic tables situated adjacent to the car park.

Checklist: score 2 points for each

1. A bridleway sign
2. Some stinging nettles
3. A pigeon
4. An oak leaf
5. Goalposts – look on a playing field
6. Some picnic tables
7. A seagull
8. Some wild poppies in a field
9. A telephone box
10. A rabbit
11. A church
12. A footpath sign pointing to Chelmondiston

Total Score _____

The Butt & Oyster, Pin Mill

The Walk

⇨ Leave the car park, turn left and make your way down the road towards the River Orwell.

☺ On your right is a well-known public house, which has existed here, in different forms since the mid-sixteenth century.

Q1 What is the name of the public house?

Score 2 points.

☺ Look to the water's edge, known as "the hard". Can you see any old sailing barges here?

⇨ Pass the public toilets and Pin Mill Common on the left and proceed ahead. After about 75 metres with the water in front, turn left by a public footpath sign and go up a slight incline. Look for details on a sailing club-house wall on the right.

Q2 What do the letters PMSC represent?

Score 3 points.

⇨ Turn right by a sign indicating cycle route South Suffolk B to join a bridleway with a hedge either side. Carry on walking parallel with the river on the right.

☺ Before passing through a kissing gate, look for a badge on the gatepost.

Q3 What is the full name of the route you are now walking?
    Suffolk Coast & _____ Path.

Score 2 points.

⇨ Continue ahead with a wire fence and hedge on the right. Stay on this sandy path and after about 150 metres look for a gap in the hedge and a boat moored on the bank.

☺ Take a closer look at the boat and the name painted on the side at the front.

Q4 What is the name of the firm?

Score 3 points.

⇨ Carry on and pass through a small spinney and a large oak tree to continue on a well-defined path in front. Bear right beside a footpath sign and skirt a wooded area on the left.

☺ Do not be tempted to walk over soft ground to the water's edge. It is dangerous to do so and you might get bogged down and need to be rescued!

⇨ The path now swings slightly to the left into a soft earth area, especially so after inclement weather conditions. You should be able to pick up the path fairly easily here.

☺ Shortly you will see some sailing dinghies stored behind a hedge. Would you like the chance to learn and sail one? The path now passes in front of a sailing clubhouse situated just away from the water's edge.

Q5 Who does the building belong to?

Score 2 points.

⇨ You have now arrived at Woolverstone Marina. Go over a short stretch of tarmac and swing left up a concrete road.

☺ The building on the right, steeped in historic intrigue, is known as the Cat House. It is said to have been the home of Margaret Catchpole, an Ipswich servant girl who fell in love with smuggler Will Laud. When smuggling was rife on the river, legend has it that a white china cat was placed in a window to warn smugglers that the excise men were on duty.

⇨ Continue along the rising road with boats in various states of repair positioned on either side. On your right is a chandlery store where sailors can buy items such as cordage, canvas and general groceries. About halfway up the hill look for a footpath sign, which may be partially hidden in some undergrowth. Turn left, go down some steps and bear right. Follow the marker posts through an area of vegetation and finally emerge onto a playing field. You may come across some goalposts and nets here and perhaps a local game of football taking place. Skirt Woolverstone church on the left, continue to bear left and join a surfaced road on the

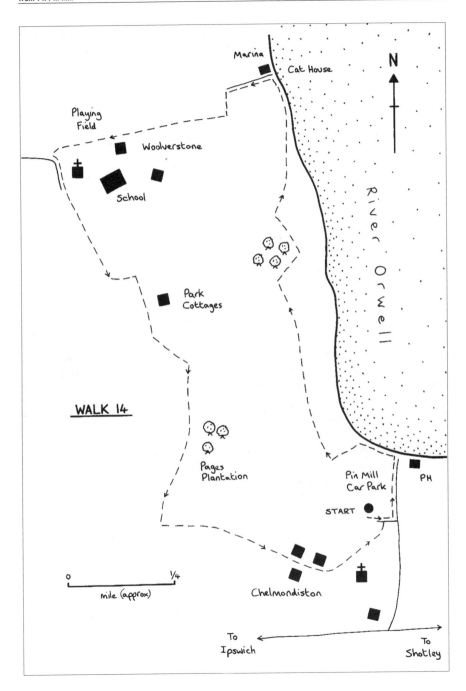

Marina

Cat House

N

Playing
Field

Woolverstone

School

River Orwell

Park
Cottages

WALK 14

Pages
Plantation

Pin Mill
Car Park

PH

START

0   1/4

mile (approx)

Chelmondiston

To
Ipswich

To
Shotley

right. Stay on the road and after about 20 metres continue to the second stile marked 'Public Footpath Chelmondiston'. Cross the stile and enter some pastureland. Carry on ahead, pass over a school driveway and cross two more stiles in quick succession.

☺   Members of the Berners family built the impressive building of Woolverstone Hall in the Palladian Style in 1776. It is now occupied by the Ipswich School for Girls. Quite an impressive place for a school, eh?

⇨   Follow a field-edge path straight ahead and bear left when meeting another path coming from the right. After passing a high hedge at Park Cottages the path shortly bears right. Ignore a path going left and right and continue downhill, passing Pages Plantation on the left. Look to the right and find an isolated cottage.

Q6 What is the name of the cottage?

Score 2 points.

⇨   Just past the cottage, turn left onto a bridleway and continue along a field-edge. Eventually you will pass between a housing estate on the right and a sports field on the left. Cross Woodlands Road and after about 150 metres bear left to join a surfaced road. Continue ahead with Chelmondiston church appearing in front. Just before reaching a road junction, turn left onto an unsurfaced road and cross a stile at the far end to enter some pasture. Walk down the sloping pasture and cross another stile in the bottom right-hand corner. Turn left and the car park is beside you. If you fancy taking a picnic, there are some tables nearby.

Now add up your score.

More than 30   An excellent score!

20 – 30   You're getting there!

Less than 20   Where have you been looking?

Walk 15. Polstead

Mention the small village of Polstead and most people associate it with a gruesome murder which caused a sensation at the time and has been a subject of fascination ever since. Briefly, local farmer's son William Corder was eventually tried and hanged for the murder of single mother Maria Marten, whose body was discovered in a red barn in 1828. Maria had left her home at Polstead to meet Corder, her lover, in the barn but suspicions were aroused when her family heard nothing from them for months. Her stepmother dreamt that she had seen Marten's buried in the red barn and eventually her shallow grave was discovered. Corder was arrested in London and later confessed to shooting Maria. The original red barn has long disappeared but the walk does cover a stretch known as the Red Barn footpath and later passes the thatched cottage where Maria once lived in Marten's Lane. The full story of Maria Marten and a short history of Polstead, complete with a footpath map of the village, is contained in a small booklet obtainable from the village community shop.

Elsewhere the walk passes some attractive cottages and gardens before arriving at the village green. Later, the route goes through a delightful area of woodland, an unusual earth road with a section of holly hedge and some undulating pastureland.

Starting Point: Polstead is 5 miles SW of Hadleigh. Take the A1071 and follow the signpost to Polstead.

Parking: By a large duck pond in Polstead. Grid Reference: 990 381.

Distance: 3.5 miles.

Map: OS Explorer No 196 Sudbury, Hadleigh & Dedham Vale.

Terrain: Good paths but with one or two up and downhill sections.

Pushchairs: Not suitable except in and around Polstead village.

Public Toilets: None on route.

Refreshments: The Cock Inn on the village green serves a wide menu and has a small garden where children are welcomed. Light refreshments are obtainable from the village community shop.

Checklist: score 2 points for each

1. Some ducks on a pond
2. Some thistles
3. An oak leaf
4. Some overhead power cables
5. A thatched cottage
6. A farm tractor
7. Some bales of hay
8. A row of young trees
9. A flock of sheep
10. Some geese in a meadow
11. An old tree stump
12. A paddock fence

Total Score _____

The Walk

⇨ Start at the large duck pond where mallard can often be seen paddling across the water. You may even see a kingfisher here. Walk with the pond on the left to reach a wooden seat just in front.

Q1 What date is inscribed on the backrest of the seat?

Score 2 points.

⇨ Turn left to follow the road and start to climb a hill through the village, admiring the pretty cottages and gardens on the way. About halfway up the hill, turn left on a narrow byway to reach the village green.

Q2 On your left is a shop. What is the title of the shop?

Score 2 points.

⇨ Carry on straight ahead along Heath Road and after about 200 metres turn left and head for Dollops Wood in front.

☺ You'll enjoy going through the wood, looking out for yellow arrows on tree trunks to guide you.

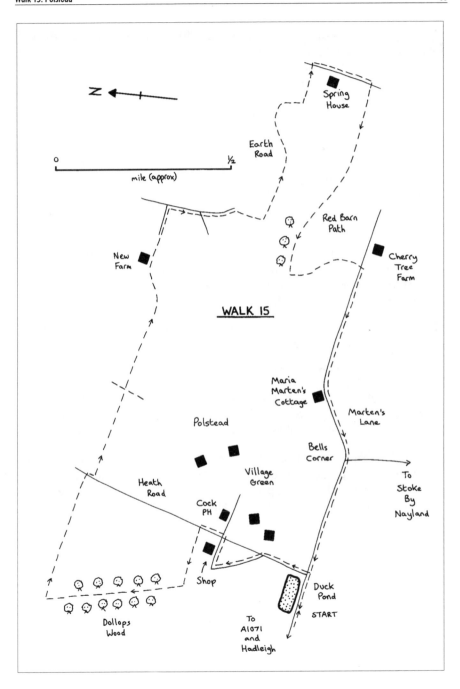

⇨ Go down a steep-ish embankment, turn right at the bottom and follow an undulating path, with the odd boggy patch. At the far end of the wood go through a kissing gate and turn right with a barn in front. Go through another kissing gate and after about 30 metres take a left fork which takes you up a slight incline with a stile at the top. Continue on a broad grassy path and turn right when you reach Heath Road again. After about 150 metres turn left to join a path with a hedge on the left. Keep beside the hedge and carry on straight ahead when you reach a four-finger signpost. Pass a thatched cottage with traditional pink-washed colours on the left and soon a horse paddock. Stay on the path as it bears left and shortly go past a large house, also on the left. Carry straight on and continue through a farmyard at New House Farm to join a concrete driveway.

☺ Notice how the landowner has planted some young trees beside the driveway to improve the landscape. At the far end of the driveway, turn right and walk along a road to reach a signpost. Look carefully at the directions.

Q3 What according to the sign is the mileage to the villages of Shelley and Layham?

Score 1 point for each answer.

⇨ Carry straight on and where the road bears left, turn right onto a grassy path. Follow the latter and just before reaching some pasture turn left (not marked) into an old earth road which may be boggy in places.

☺ Local people used this sort of road long before surface roads were introduced. Nowadays it is still used by horses, which often churn the mud up with their hooves. Note the stretch of a lovely holly hedge at the far end.

⇨ Exit the earth road, turn right, pass Spring House and take the next turning right over a stile. Walk down some pasture beside a paddock fence and cross three stiles in quick succession. Go to the left of a barn and continue over a walkway before turning right onto the waymarked path.

☺ You can usually see cattle on some pasture beside the path. Score 3 bonus points if you see a herd of six or more.

⇨ Follow the path round and eventually ignore a path going right.

Village sign and green, Polstead

Carry on for a further 15 metres to cross a stile and enter a grassy area. Keep well to the left and head up a rising path to eventually turn right at the junction with Marten's Lane. Polstead is also well known for its cherry trees.

Q4 Look to the left. What is the name of the farm associated with a fruit?

Score 2 points.

▷ Continue down Marten's Lane and look out for Maria Marten's cottage about halfway down. At a road junction, Bells Corner, go straight over. Continue along the road for about another 200 metres and the duck pond will shortly appear on the right.

Now let's add up the score.

More than 28   Well done – keep it up!

20 – 28   You're getting there!

Under 20   Better luck on the next walk!

Walk 16. Sizewell

This walk starts from Sizewell, a small fishing village that often hits the headlines over safety in the nuclear power industry. A walk along a cliff top, with the sound of waves from the North Sea breaking on the shingle beach below, brings you to the unusual holiday village of Thorpeness. The village was created from 1911 onwards by an eccentric local landowner, Captain Stuart Ogilvie. The village had (and still does) a golf course, artificial lake (referred to as the Meare) and mock-Tudor architecture. You can visit The Meare (just off route), hire a rowing boat if you like and explore the small islands and natural wildlife.

Elsewhere, the route takes you along broad sandy tracks in an area appropriately known as the Sandlings and over heathland before returning to the beach at Sizewell. Just north of Sizewell, but not on route, two nuclear power stations can be seen. If you have sufficient time and energy left over from the walk, the coastal path provides a good vantage-point should you want a close-up view.

Starting Point: Go to Leiston and follow signs to Sizewell. Continue to the end of the road by the beach.

Parking: Public car park at Sizewell Beach. Grid Reference: 476 628.

Distance: 5 miles.

Map: OS Explorer No 212 Woodbridge and Saxmundham.

Terrain: Mostly walking cliff top and sandy paths

Pushchairs: Suitable only along some sections of the beach and in Thorpeness.

Public Toilets: Sizewell Beach.

Refreshments: There is a tea-room on the beach at Sizewell, which does meals, teas and light refreshments. Phone 01728 831108 for opening times. Also there is a shop and tea-room at the Meare, The Dolphin pub at Thorpeness serves excellent food and drink and welcomes children.

Checklist: score 2 points for each

1. Some fishing boats.
2. A caravan park.
3. A water standpipe and bowl.
4. Pebbles in a stone wall.
5. A seagull.
6. Some wooden steps and a handrail.
7. A rook.
8. A farm cottage with the name of a tree.
9. A thatched barn.
10. Notice "Caution – flying golf balls."
11. A conservation area.
12. Wrought iron gates.

Total Score _____

Windmill, Thorpeness

The Walk

▷ Leave the car park, walk out towards the beach and turn right to enter a broad ride between the beach and some grass.

☺ Take a look behind you and you will see the Sizewell A and B nuclear power stations further along the coast.

Q1 What is the colour of the dome of Sizewell B power station?

Score 2 points.

▷ Keep forward and pass a row of black weatherboarded cottages on the right. As you approach a large white house on the cliff top, climb up the cliff on a grassy path and pass the house on the right. Keep going ahead and shortly go under a tunnel belonging to Sizewell Hall. Stay on the cliff top path passing through areas of bramble and bracken overlooking the beach below.

☺ What are the sea conditions like today? Is it calm or is it rough with large waves breaking on the beach? Can you see any gulls flying over the water?

▷ Ignore a track going right just by some blocks of concrete. Continue along the sandy path, which gradually descends to join the beach.

☺ Now keep your eyes skinned for part of a World War II defence relic – a concrete pillbox.

Q2 Facing the sea, how many open slits does it have, including a partially closed one?

Score 2 points.

▷ After passing some houses on the cliff top, the latter gradually recedes. Continue along a section of shingle beach and look for a large block of houses forming a kind of semicircle facing the sea. Immediately before it turn right onto a marked path with the sea behind you to enter Thorpeness village. When you meet a road in front follow it round left, and then right to reach the Dolphin pub. Turn left along a road named The Winlands and in about 100 metres turn right into Upland Road. (If you wish to visit The Meare, it is just in front).

▷ Continue along the unmade Upland Road and look to your left when passing some cottage gardens.

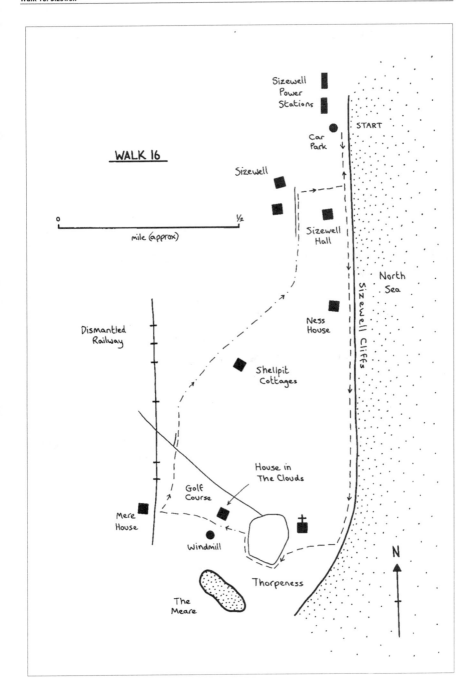

WALK 16

Sizewell
Power
Stations

Car
Park

START

Sizewell

Sizewell
Hall

0   ½

mile (approx)

North
Sea

Dismantled
Railway

Ness
House

Sizewell Cliffs

Shellpit
Cottages

House in
The Clouds

Golf
Course

Mere
House

Windmill

Thorpeness

The
Meare

N

Q3 What is the number painted on a small boat filled with flowers?

Score 3 points.

☺ On the right is a most unusual building known as The House In The Clouds. Just ahead of you is a windmill. The windmill, originally a corn grinding mill, was converted to pump water when it was moved from nearby Aldringham to Thorpeness in 1922. Rather than spoil the horizon with a huge water tank to contain what was being pumped by the windmill, Captain Ogilvie, whom we met earlier, boarded over the metal structure and brilliantly disguised it as a house. The house is now a holiday home and the windmill acts as a visitor centre.

Q4 Take a good look at the house. What object stands beside the right-hand side wall?

Score 2 points.

⇨ Carry on past the windmill and spot the flagstaff belonging to the Thorpeness Golf Club.

Q5 What emblems are shown on the flag?

Score 3 points.

⇨ Continue for 10 metres on a surfaced road and where the road bends left, go straight ahead as marked between hedgerows. With the Meare on the left, stay on this path which skirts the golf course and reach Mere Cottage.

Q6 What is the date shown on the cottage?

Score 2 points.

⇨ Turn right and pass the cottage on the left. Continue ahead and in 100 metres, where the lane goes half left, go straight on to reach a main-tenance yard. Large mowers to help keep the golf course in trim are sometimes parked here. Turn left and continue on a gravel track to meet a road. Cross the road and continue on a concrete surface, which soon becomes a dusty track. In 250 metres, keep on the main track where it bends half right. Carry on along this broad track and after 300 metres pass some isolated buildings known as Shellpit Cottages.

☺ The track may seem dull and never ending but there are usually birds and small mammals to identify.

☺ Score 3 bonus points if you spot a bird of prey such as a kestrel or a sparrowhawk.

⇨ Carry on for about another 400 metres and ignore all turnings left until you reach a track coming from the right. Turn left to continue on a track which later becomes a road taking you to the entrance to Sizewell Hall.

☺ A notice on the gates tells you what activities go on at the Hall.

Q7 What do the initial letters CCC represent on the noticeboard?

Score 2 points.

⇨ Turn sharp right and head in the direction of the sea. Do not deviate from the path that passes a caravan and camping site on the right. When you reach the cliff top, turn left and retrace your steps along the beach back to your start point.

Well done! Now it's score time again ...

More than 30   You're the tops!

25 – 30   A good effort

Under 25   Where were you looking?

Extra congratulations if you scored the bonus points!

Walk 17. Southwold

The small coastal resort of Southwold – which has been awarded a 'blue flag' for its clean beaches – has lots of interesting things to do and see. There are several reminders of the town's nautical tradition in terms of military defence and longshore fishing. The harbour path, which runs parallel with the River Blyth, has pleasure craft and fishing boats moored alongside a long line of slipways and jetties. Opposite the river are sheds where locally caught fresh fish is on sale. The lonely Buss Creek marshes, which provide a rear view of Southwold, are strewn with rushes and reeds. Horses and cattle can often be seen grazing here. During the walk you can stroll along Southwold's pier, over 500 metres long and the first pier extension in Britain for over 50 years. From the cliff-top path, a short detour leads to a close-up view of the inland lighthouse, standing amongst some cottages. Other interesting sights include Adnams' Brewery and St Edmunds church. Pop inside the Sailors' Reading Room and find out about Southwold's seafaring past from a collection of old photographs and artefacts. The six cannon pointing out to the sea at Gun Hill will fascinate youngsters of all ages. Their origin is unclear although they may have been part of an armoury supplied to Southwold during the early seventeenth century to protect the town and ships anchored in the bay from enemy fire. A couple of miniature cannon stand either side of a mast in St James's Green.

Starting Point: Southwold is situated off the A12 just about a mile north of Blythburgh. From here take the A1095 to Southwold, go through the town centre and follow the signs to Southwold Harbour.

Parking: Pay and display at Southwold Harbour. Grid Reference: 504 749.

Distance: 4.5 miles.

Map: OS Explorer No 231 Southwold & Bungay.

Terrain: Good paths, mostly on the level, but boggy stretches across the marshes.

Pushchairs: Suitable only for the harbour and town areas.

Public Toilets: At the harbour, beside the pier, along the cliff top and in Ferry Road.

Refreshments: Tea-rooms along the Harbour Road, beside and on the pier. Similar establishments can be found in the town itself along with a selection of public houses, which welcome children.

Checklist: score 2 points for each

1. A bridge over the river
2. Some swallows
3. A derelict brick water pumping mill; clue – look left next to the river for this one
4. Some buttercups
5. A distant lighthouse
6. A moorhen
7. A fisherman's umbrella
8. A model yacht pond
9. A Union Jack flag – there could be more than one
10. A yacht out to sea
11. Some pebbles on the beach
12. An ice cream stall

Total Score _____

Beach huts, Southwold

The Walk

⇨ Leave the car park with the North Sea behind you and walk along the harbour path with the River Blyth on the left.

☺ Soon, look right as you pass a series of small sheds, which sell
_   fresh fish.

Q1 From names on the sheds, complete the following blanks:

Willies _____

Happy _____

Score 1 point for each.

⇨ Carry on straight-ahead and reach the Harbour Inn on the right. Look for a plaque on the wall indicating the height reached by a disastrous flood.

Q2 In which year did the flood take place?

Score 2 points.

☺ Shortly you may come across some youngsters by the riverbank with a net, line and a bucket. More than likely they will be fishing for crabs.

☺ If you see some crabs in a bucket, in a jar, or on a line – score a bonus 3 points.

⇨ Keep going ahead and follow the path to the top of a flood protection wall. When you reach a bridge going over the river, carry straight on over a stile. Just as the river bends away left, the path now continues beside Buss Creek, a narrow water channel. Stay on a raised path beside the creek, which takes you through a large area of rushes and reeds around the back of Southwold. When you reach a four-fingered signpost, cross two stiles and carry on straight ahead with a water course on the left.

☺ Keep your eyes open to spot some horses or cattle, which graze the marshes here.

⇨ Maintain direction for about 1000 metres and meet a white-painted bridge at right angles. Cross over Mights Road beside the bridge and keep forward on a well-defined path over more marshland. Ignore a path

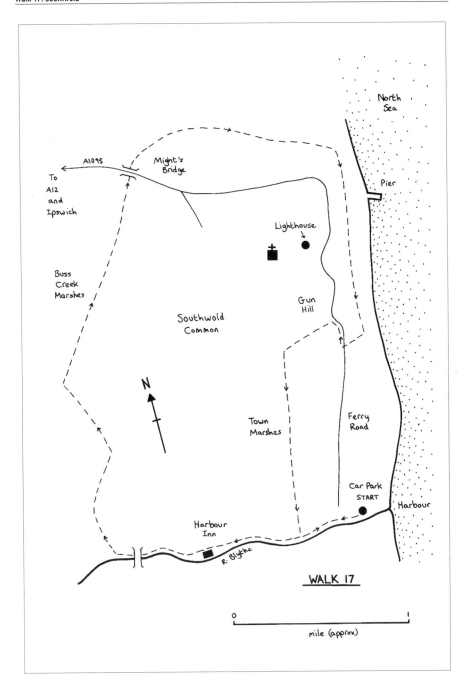

North
Sea

A1095

Might's
Bridge

Pier

To
A12
and
Ipswich

Lighthouse

✝ ■   ●

Buss
Creek
Marshes

Southwold
Common

Gun
Hill

N

Town
Marshes

Ferry
Road

Car Park
START

Harbour

Harbour
Inn

R. Blythe

WALK 17

0   1

mile (approx)

coming from the right and continue ahead. In the distance, and getting closer, is a row of multi-coloured shapes.

Q3 What do you think these shapes represent?

Score 2 points.

⇨　Carry on as before and shortly walk between the creek on the left and a lake on the right. Come off the path when you reach a beachside car park. Turn right and continue between the car park and a model yacht pond.

☺　You are now approaching Southwold pier on the left. Take a look on the pier (free admission) and find a most unusual water clock.

Q4 At what times does the clock perform? Clue – details are beside the clock.

Score 2 points.

⇨　Come off the pier, turn left and join a cliff top path with the beach and sea below. Continue to St James's Green on the right, a triangular piece of green where a cannon stands either side of a mast. From here, make a short detour if you wish to view the lighthouse and Adnams' Brewery. Otherwise, stay on the path and reach the Southwold Sailors' Reading Room (1864).

Q5 What is displayed on the right-hand side of the entrance?

Score 2 points.

⇨　Walk past a grassed area on the right and carry straight on. The path soon drops almost to beach level and then quickly rises up to Gun Hill.

☺　On the left you will find a beacon. Look at the small plate attached to the pole.

Q6 On which date was the beacon lit?

Score 2 points.

☺　Take a close look at the six cannon pointing out to sea. Can you imagine them being fired in their heyday? The nearby small lifeboat museum is worth a peep inside if it's open.

⇨ Continue to where the path almost peters out and turn right onto another path, which leads to Ferry Road. Turn right here, pass some toilets and walk along a paved area for about 150 metres. Where the road bends right, turn sharp left at a circular walk sign and continue along a broad path. Keep following the path until you reach the river in front. Turn left here and take the harbour path back to your start point.

Now add up your score. Well done if you scored the bonus points.

More than 30   Excellent observation!

20 – 30   Pretty good!

Under 20   Never mind – try another walk!

Walk 18. Sudbury

The market town of Sudbury has a recreational facility that few other places can boast of. On its doorstep are over 200 acres of lush pasture that form what is known as the Sudbury Common Lands. Footpaths cross the area and visitors are invited to explore the lovely water meadows bounded on one side by the River Stour. The meadows have a long history, going back to the 11th century, and were first mentioned in the Domesday survey of 1086. Under grazing rights acquired in about 1260, the Freemen of Sudbury can graze their horses and cattle here. The meadows have never been subjected to intensive farming and grazing is set to continue in future years. As a result, you are likely to have to share this peaceful and tranquil setting with rare breeds of Galloway and Highland cattle – they are unlikely to harm you unless you get close and provoke them in any way. The famous landscape and portrait painter, Thomas Gainsborough, Sudbury's most famous son, would have wandered through these meadows and hedgerows, which later inspired his early paintings. His father's house, where Gainsborough was born, stands in Gainsborough Street and is now a museum. Children are welcomed to discover more about the artist's life and work and look at some of his paintings and drawings which are kept there. The museum is only a short distance from the Market Hill where a bronze statue of Gainsborough stands. From the picnic site, a gravel path takes you to Sudbury by way of a disused railway line known as the Valley Walk. You can make a detour into the town or carry on through the meadows by the riverside, pass historic Brundon Mill and return to the car park.

Starting Point: Rodbridge picnic site is signposted off the A134 at Rodbridge Corner 2 miles north of Sudbury.

Parking: Rodbridge picnic site. Grid Reference: 853 438.

Distance: 5 miles.

Map: OS Explorer No 196 Sudbury, Hadleigh & Dedham Vale.

Terrain: Good paths and mostly on level ground.

Pushchairs: Useable on the entire route apart from embankment steps and longish grass here and there.

Public Toilets: At the picnic site.

Refreshments: Picnic tables at Rodbridge. In Sudbury, take your pick from a selection of pubs and tea shops around the Market Hill area.

Checklist: score 2 points for each

1. Some picnic tables
2. A brick bridge
3. A cyclist on the Valley Walk
4. A dragonfly
5. Sign – South Suffolk Route A
6. A silver birch tree
7. Horses in a paddock
8. Footpath sign to Ballingdon
9. Red lifebelt holder
10. A weir beside a river
11. A swan
12. A rabbit hole

Total Score _____

The Walk

⇨   Come out of the picnic site and continue down the road you just came along to reach a road bridge. This bridge over the River Stour forms the boundary between Suffolk and Essex.

Q1 As you approach the bridge, what is the speed limit permitted for vehicles crossing the bridge?

Score 2 points.

⇨   Cross the bridge and turn left beside the entrance to the Valley Walk. Continue ahead on a gravel path. After a while you will notice that the hedgerows now tend to be overgrown and overhang at the top. About 30 metres after passing over steel bridge, turn left and continue on a path with a hedge on the left. At the next gate ignore a path going straight ahead and instead turn right to follow a track and shortly reach a farm on the left.

Q2 What is the name of the farm?

Score 2 points.

⇨ Keep forward and follow the track round to reach a brick bridge. Go down some steps cut in the bank and rejoin the Valley Walk.

You're now getting closer to the outskirts of Sudbury. Look in front and slightly left and see if you can spot two church towers in the landscape as well as the white-painted Mill Hotel.

⇨ Keep going ahead on the former track bed where steam trains once ran. Now look to your right through a series of small gaps in the hedgerow and you should see the outline of a sports stadium.

Q3 From what you can see, which sport do you think is played here?

Score 3 points.

⇨ Carry on ahead and soon you will almost be in Sudbury. Continue straight on for the Kingfisher swimming pool and railway station. Otherwise, soon after passing over another steel bridge, turn left down an embankment and left again at the bottom. Go forward for 20 metres and stop beside an old pumping station on the right.

Q4 Look carefully at the brickwork. What date is shown amongst the bricks?

Score 3 points.

⇨ Go ahead through a kissing gate where a notice welcomes you to the Sudbury Common Lands and nature reserve. Notice how the River Stour has branched away into narrow channels amongst the meadows before continuing on its way again.

⇨ Carry on across a meadow and aim for a bridge over the river in front. Turn right over the bridge and walk towards the Mill Hotel almost straight ahead. Turn left here and continue on a narrow path, which leads to some gardens and a picnic area.

☺ Nearby is an almost oval-shaped model pond.

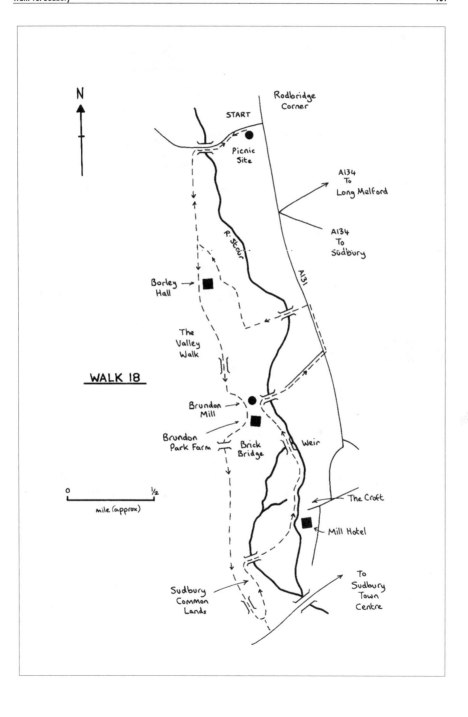

Q5 What is the name on the side of the pond?

Score 2 points.

⇨ If you want to make a short detour to visit Gainsborough's house and statue (about 10 minutes walk) turn right over the adjacent bridge and continue along Croft Street and Gaol Lane to the Market Hill. Otherwise, continue ahead and re-enter the Common Lands. You are now walking across the delightful sounding Great and Little Fullingpit Meadows.

☺ During the spring and summer months the meadows are ablaze with buttercups and other wild flowers. Are there any cattle around today, The statue of Thomas Gainsborough some rare breeds perhaps? Can you identify any? Score 3 bonus points if you see one with a shaggy coat and long horns.

⇨ Shortly, veer left and follow a path, which crosses a bridge with metal railings beside a weir. Keep forward and soon you will see a brick wall with Brundon Hall tucked away behind it. Follow the direction of the wall, go through a metal kissing gate and emerge by the Hall entrance. Bear left here and shortly afterwards swing right to pass the bordered Brundon Mill on the left. Go over a bridge, bear left and follow a surfaced lane to the junction with the Sudbury and Long Melford road. Turn left here and walk along a paved area.

☺ Keep looking right for a road by a housing estate opposite.

Q6 What is the name of the road associated with a poet of Canterbury fame?

Score 2 points.

⇨ Shortly after passing a hotel, turn left onto an earth path by a foot-path sign, which leads to a timber bridge. Cross the bridge, go through a kissing gate and carry on straight-ahead. At the far side, go through another kissing gate and cross a bridge. Swing right and keep beside a hedge on the right and head for Borley Hall in front. Just before reaching a brick building turn right through a pedestrian gate. Bear slightly left and then follow a narrow path beside a high garden wall, which leads to an entrance drive. Walk down the drive to a junction and turn right onto the Valley Walk. Retrace your steps back to the picnic site.

Well done – now add up your score, remembering to add the bonus if you got it!

More than 30   An excellent score!

20 – 30   A pretty good try!

Under 20   Look more carefully next time!

Walk 19. Witnesham

The village of Witnesham is a scattered parish straddling the B1077 between Ipswich and Debenham. Like many of its Suffolk counterparts, Witnesham has an official circular walk, which takes you around the village. This walk follows part of that route and links up with other public rights of way should you wish to extend the walk.

During periods of really wet weather the village, which stands at the bottom of a shallow valley, is susceptible to flooding, as evidenced by two fords and the appropriately named Wash Lane. Red House Farm is an attractive building, part of which dates from about 1450. Another interesting building worth making a short detour to discover, is the 16th-century Witnesham Hall. Apparently, the timber framing was encased in red brick during remodelling in about 1842. As the name suggests, Mill Lane once had a windmill where until 1906 it stood next to Mill Cottage. A notice beside a well close to the war memorial suggests that the former has been in use for some 600 years. A handy source for washing and drinking water no doubt until piped mains finally arrived. Witnesham's most famous resident was the well-known cartoonist, Carl Giles, who, before his death, lived in the village for a number of years. Nowadays a road called Giles Way perpetuates his name.

Starting Point: Witnesham lies almost 5 miles north of Ipswich along the B1077.

Parking: Free car park situated by the village sign close to the Barley Mow public house. Grid Reference: 184 504.

Distance: 2.5 miles.

Map: OS Explorer No 211 Bury St Edmunds & Stowmarket and 197 Ipswich, Felixstowe & Harwich.

Terrain: Good paths with one or two slight up and downhill sections. Boggy patches exist in wet conditions. Wash Lane may be flooded in places during wet weather.

Pushchairs: Not suitable.

Public Toilets: None on route.

Refreshments: The Barley Mow public house welcomes families and has a small garden.

Checklist: score 2 points for each

1. A combine harvester
2. A rook
3. A telegraph pole
4. A field of corn
5. Two tall silo towers
6. A birds feather
7. Some tall poplar trees
8. A barbed wire fence
9. Some iron railings beside a ford
10. A farm cart shed
11. A well beside the road
12. A village sign

Total Score _____

The Walk

⇨ Leave the car park and head towards the street in front. Turn left and quickly right into Tuddenham Lane almost opposite. Continue uphill to reach Red House Farm on the left. Continue straight ahead along Bull Hall Lane and go through a gate at the far end.

Q1 What are the colours of a bridleway badge on the gatepost (and found elsewhere on the walk)?

Score 2 points.

☺ There is plenty of muck around here so be prepared for a whiff or two!

⇨ Bear left, go over a strip of concrete and join a concrete road with some long poultry sheds on the right at nearby Maple Tree Farm.

Q2 The sheds are all numbered. What number is the last shed that you pass?

Score 2 points.

⇨ Turn right and continue by the side of a shed and after 15 metres bear left and right to continue along a field-edge path beside a hedge. The path shortly curves left and, in about 20 metres, becomes enclosed with a hedge either side. Continue ahead beside a wire fence and shortly ignore a cross-field path going left. Follow the field-edge path to the field corner with Burnt House Farm appearing on the right. Turn left here and join a cinder track. Bear left at the bottom and shortly go past the entrance to White House Farm. Keep forward, pass a ford and continue along Wash Lane to reach the junction with the B1077.

☺   Did you find much water along the lane, or just the odd puddle? Turn left here for a short cut back to the car park. Otherwise cross straight over the road to join Church Lane and arrive at the village hall.

☺   Look for a stone set into a wall and the date 1810. With a little study, you can just about make sense of the inscription.

Q3   How was the school funded?

Score 3 points.

⇨   Go past St Mary's church and shortly reach another ford.

☺   Usually the water here is just a trickle over the road. However, if the water is deep, use the bridge on the bank to view Witnesham Hall just in front of you. Of course, if you have wellies on, you may be able to paddle through!

Q4   What is the maximum height of the flood level indicated on a nearby post?

Score 2 points.

⇨   Just before you approach the ford turn left and continue to reach a bridge. Cross over the latter and a stile to enter a meadow. Keep bearing left, go through a gate into another meadow and head up towards Manor Farm. Turn right at the farm, go through a gate and continue on a rising grassy path, which shortly runs between two fields. The path later continues with a hedge and ditch on the right. When you reach a track continue straight ahead and shortly descend Mill Lane.

☺   At the junction with the B1077 there is a war memorial beside the road.

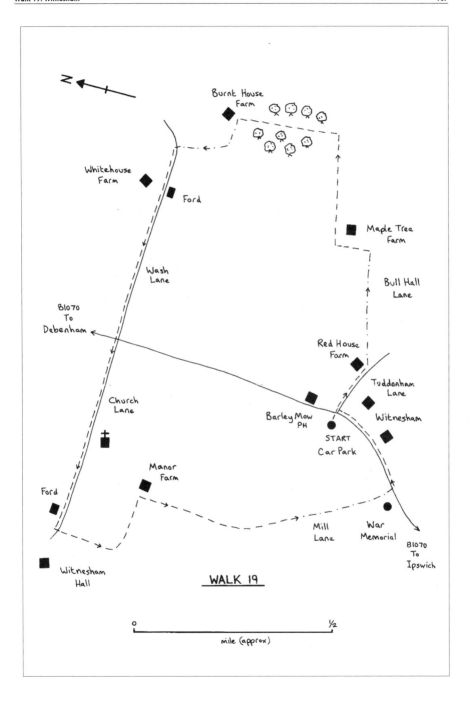

WALK 19

Witnesham Hall

Q5 Which world wars does the memorial commemorate?

Score 2 points.

➪   Turn left onto a paved area and your start point is a few metres further on.

Now add up your score.

More than 30   Extremely well done!

20 – 30   A good try!

Less than 20   Better luck next time!

Walk 20. Woodbridge

Woodbridge is an attractive town steeped in history. There is no wooden bridge as such, the name more likely has Saxon or Norse origins, meaning "Woden's Town". This walk concentrates on the river and countryside areas rather than the town itself, which can be explored later. One of the chief attractions is the 18th-century Tide Mill, an interesting example of early Industrial Revolution technology which has been completely restored and is open for all to see. Just over the river is the site of the famous burial at Sutton Hoo. Here in 625 AD a 27-metre rowing vessel was dragged from the Deben to form the resting-place of the Wuffing King Redwald. The treasures buried there were discovered in 1939 and are now on show in the British Museum.

Woodbridge sits at the top of the River Deben, which is navigable and passes through attractive countryside before entering the North Sea. The river attracts large numbers of the sailing fraternity who make use of the harbour and various repair metres. It also appeals to walkers wanting an easy stroll. A tarmac riverside path, which stretches for about half a mile, enables visitors to walk traffic-free and observe the activities on the water. At Kyson Point there are superb views of salt marshes, mudflats and historic remains of the ancient quay. Further along the riverbank you can follow the river as it flows into an area known as Martlesham Creek. In the Maidensgrove area you are welcomed to explore and take a walk through Porter's Wood.

Starting Point: Outside the railway station in Station Road. Woodbridge is 8 miles east of Ipswich; turn off the A12 and follow the signs. Woodbridge can be reached by rail on the East Suffolk Line and also by bus. Tel 0870 6082608 for further details.

Parking: Pay and Display beside the railway station in Station Road.

Distance: 4 miles.

Map: OS Explorer No 197 Ipswich, Felixstowe and Harwich.

Terrain: Surfaced path and roads. Riverbank path can be muddy in winter.

Pushchairs: Can be used along river walk for about 800 metres.

Public Toilets: Some in town centre.

Refreshments: Woodbridge has a good choice of restaurants and pubs. Mrs Piper's Restaurant, 65 Thoroughfare, and Pickwick's Restaurant and Tea Rooms, Gobbitts Yard, Thoroughfare, both welcome children and serve home-cooked meals.

Checklist: score 2 points for each

1. A theatre building
2. A sailing dinghy
3. A yacht club
4. A train
5. A black headed gull (search the mudflats for this bird)
6. Cattle in a meadow
7. A large oak tree
8. A church tower (look in the distance for this one)
9. A blackbird
10. A dog on a lead
11. Some gravestones
12. A post box

Total Score _____

The Walk

⇨ Exit the car park, go past the Riverside Theatre and turn right onto the road. After about 150 metres turn right into Tide Mill Way. Cross the railway line and look at the buildings on the left.

Q1 Which youth organisation uses a building here as its HQ?

Score 2 points.

⇨ Carry on just ahead to the Tide Mill. Have a look around the outside of the mill, which operates at various times depending on the tide. For opening times ring 01473 626618. Retrace your steps back and turn left into Riverside Walk. Follow the path, which runs beside a variety of moored boats and repair metres to a railway bridge.

☺ This area is prone to flooding at high tide, so floodgates have been installed.

The river and tide mill at Woodbridge

Q2 What is the number of the floodgate nearest the bridge?

Score 2 points.

⇨ Continue along a surfaced path with the river on the left, again with an assortment of boats moored everywhere.

☺ On your right you will soon pass the Woodbridge Cruising Club house. Look for a panel on the side of the clubhouse facing you.

Q3 What is the club's emblem?

Score 3 points.

⇨ With the river on the left, carry on ahead and soon you will leave the boat repair yards behind.

☺ On the right are water meadows, carpeted with wild flowers during the late spring and early summertime. Can you spot any buttercups or cattle grazing perhaps? Shortly, Kyson Hill an area belonging to the National Trust will come into view. Take a close look at the sign beside the path.

Q4 What is the emblem of the National Trust?

Score 2 points.

⇨ Ignore a path going right to Sandy Hill and instead take an unsurfaced path, which goes up a slight incline before bearing left down to a small strip of beach. (If the tide is high here, retrace your steps back and turn left into Sandy Lane. You then rejoin the walk again at Broom Heath). 50 metres after passing a raised seat, bear right and join a narrow path with a wooden fence on the left. Away to the left is water that eventually flows into Martlesham Creek.

☺ Have a look for the intricate patterns on the mudflats, visible when the tide is out.

⇨ Where the fence ends turn right and go up a bank. You are now walking on part of the local Fynn Valley route. When you finally arrive at a T-junction of footpaths going left and right, take the latter. Continue along a narrow path, pass a sewerage treatment works to reach a junction with a minor road. Turn right, go under a rail bridge and proceed up a steadily rising road for about 600 metres.

☺ Do you have any refreshments? You certainly deserve a drink or whatever after that long climb!

⇨ Just before turning right into Broom Heath, look for a yellow and green sign indicating another form of transport.

Q5 What does the sign depict? (If your legs are tired, you may wish you had one).

Score 2 points.

⇨ Turn right into an area known as Broom Heath and continue on a surfaced road with mature trees on either side. Where the road bends right, turn sharp left and join Sandy Lane.

☺ On your right, a notice board tells you that visitors are welcome to explore the attractive woodland known as Porter's Wood. Why not have a quick look round if you have the time?

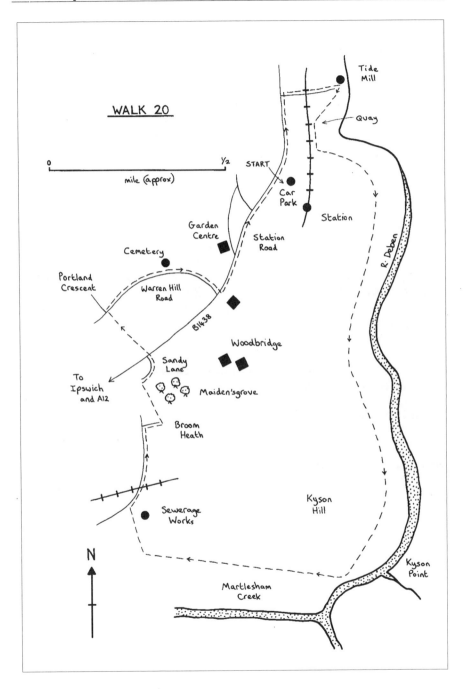

WALK 20

0   ½
mile (approx)

Tide Mill

Quay

START

Car Park

Station

Garden Centre

Station Road

Cemetery

R. Deben

Portland Crescent

Warren Hill Road

B1438

Woodbridge

Sandy Lane

To Ipswich and A12

Maiden'sgrove

Broom Heath

Sewerage Works

Kyson Hill

N

Kyson Point

Martlesham Creek

Q6 Who does the woodland belong to? (The answer is on the notice board).

Score 3 points.

⇨ Continue to skirt the wood and shortly turn right onto a metalled surface. Turn right again at the main road and continue for about 15 metres. Cross the road with care and go up some concrete steps cut into the bank opposite.

Q7 As you walk up the steps, count the number of metal handrails.

Score 3 points.

⇨ Carry on along a path running between some rear gardens and an assortment of hedgerows to reach a road opposite Portland Crescent. Turn right here into Warren Hill Road and pass a cemetery on the left as you walk down the hill. At the junction with the main road, turn left and soon pass Notcutts Garden Centre in Cumberland Street. Cross the road and join Station Road, pass a swimming pool and your start point is just ahead of you.

Now, how did you score?

More than 30   Very well done!

20 – 30   A good attempt.

Under 20   Try again.

Answers to Questions

Walk 1. Barham & Baylham

Q1 Gipping Angling Preservation Society
Q2 The Chequers
Q3 10 mph – although the sign looks unofficial
Q4 White and Wheat
Q5 Track laying vehicles

Walk 2. Beyton

Q1 Four
Q2 2000
Q3 Quaker Farm
Q4 Oak Tree
Q5 Nil. However, some may have been added since the route was originally walked!

Walk 3. Clare

Q1 The Stour Valley Railway closed in 1967
Q2 A brick-arched bridge
Q3 A cockerel
Q4 A chevron
Q5 Essex

Walk 4. East Bergholt

Q1 Hatts – apparently straw hats were made locally during the Victorian era
Q2 1776
Q3 Time – very true!
Q4 John Constable – need I say!
Q5 Two – Dedham (in front) and Stratford (right)
Q6 1802

Walk 5. Eye

Q1 1821-1886
Q2 A "love seat". I'm not sure whether this one is used or not!
Q3 January 1998 Suffolk Wildlife Winter Tree Festival
Q4 Forty shillings – a lot of money in those days! Although I suspect the plate has been removed from elsewhere.
Q5 Wellington – the Duke who fought at the battle of Waterloo and who gave his name to Wellington boots.

Walk 6. Felixstowe – Landguard Point

Q1 Stinking Goose Foot – phew!
Q2 Around 1718
Q3 Port of Felixstowe
Q4 Over 100

Walk 7. Gazeley, Dalham & Moulton

Q1 Three. White.
Q2 Axe head and handle
Q3 A metal frame – presumably to keep cattle away from nibbling the trunk
Q4 Four feet
Q5 A restored windmill
Q6 A fish – appropriate for St Peter's church
Q7 Four

Walk 8. Hadleigh

Q1 Royal Bank of Scotland. 1000 mileposts have been funded.
Q2 Pond Hall
Q3 The National Grid PLC
Q4 Osborne Hall
Q5 Hadleigh United play football here
Q6 St Mary's church – flint. The Guildhall – timber. Deanery Tower – brick.

Walk 9. Harleston, Shelland & Onehouse

Q1 Deer
Q2 Three
Q3 A water channel – possibly part of an original moat
Q4 Horse, sheep and cow
Q5 Ash
Q6 8 ft 6 in (2.6 metres)

Walk 10. Hoxne

Q1 1844
Q2 Five – did you count them all?
Q3 A solar panel
Q4 A weather vane
Q5 Coach
Q6 AD 870

Walk 11. Lavenham

Q1 The Guildhall
Q2 PAN
Q3 Slough Farm
Q4 Lavenham Cricket Club
Q5 141 feet (43 metres)

Walk 12. Needham Market

Q1 Litter
Q2 1st Needham Market Scout Group
Q3 Swimming in the river
Q4 8 ft 3 in (2.5 metres)
Q5 SM 1718
Q6 St John the Baptist
Q7 1846

Walk 13. Orwell Country Park

Q1 1995
Q2 The year 2000 – did you spot it on one of the sculptures?
Q3 Red
Q4 White – unless it's changed colour since!
Q5 The bridge is 4218 ft long – 1278 metres!

Walk 14. Pin Mill

Q1 Butt and Oyster
Q2 Pin Mill Sailing Club – easy wasn't it!
Q3 Heaths
Q4 E Packard
Q5 Royal Harwich Yacht Club
Q6 Longwood Cottage

Walk 15. Polstead

Q1 1992
Q2 Polstead Community Shop
Q3 Two miles and two and a half miles respectively
Q4 Cherry Tree Farm

Walk 16. Sizewell

Q1 White
Q2 Two – presumably positioned to deter the enemy advancing up the beach

Q3 Seven. I hope the flowers are still in bloom!
Q4 A red telephone box
Q5 A dolphin and the letter T
Q6 1882
Q7 Christian Conference Centre

Walk 17. Southwold
Q1 Plaice and Soles – get it?
Q2 1953
Q3 Beach Huts
Q4 On the hour and half hour – did you get to hear it?
Q5 An anchor and chain
Q6 31st Dec 1999

Walk 18. Sudbury
Q1 15 miles per hour
Q2 Brundon Park Farm
Q3 Football – you might have caught sight of the goalposts!
Q4 1903 – did you spot it?
Q5 Mill Acre
Q6 Chaucer

Walk 19. Witnesham
Q1 Blue and green
Q2 Number 1
Q3 By voluntary subscription
Q4 4 ft 6 in (1.4 metres)
Q5 World Wars I and II

Walk 20. Woodbridge
Q1 Woodbridge Sea Scouts
Q2 Floodgate No 5
Q3 A galleon
Q4 Oak leaf or acorn
Q5 A bicycle
Q6 The Woodland Trust

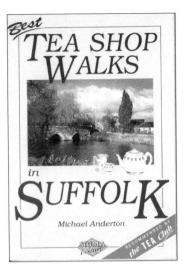